BE A
WEALTHY
THERAPIST

*Finally, You Can Make a Living
While Making a Difference*

CASEY TRUFFO

PUBLISHED BY:

MP Press, A division of
Femme Osage Publishing
1301 Colby Drive
Saint Peters, Missouri, USA 63376
www.FemmeOsagePublishing.com
Publisher@FemmeOsagePublishing.com

Printed in the United States of America

ISBN: 978-1-934509-06-7

Library of Congress Control Number: 2007934884

First Printing 2007

Author Contact:
Casey L. Truffo
2212 DuPont Drive, Suite I
Irvine, CA 92612
United States

(949) 309-2590
Casey@BeAWealthyTherapist.com
www.BeAWealthyTherapist.com

This book is dedicated to Bob – my date for life.

Table of Contents

The Love is Free

There is a parable about a kindly psychiatrist treating a very depressed and lonely woman.

Through tears, the client tells the therapist, "I don't like that I have to pay you to love me." And the psychiatrist says, "You pay me for my education, my efforts, my time, and my commitment. The love is free."

For the last several years I have worked with therapists, coaches and other healers in private practices who dearly love their clients and their work. In fact they love them so much that sometimes these clinicians forget they need to be paid. Or they feel guilty about charging a fee. Others want to share their gifts with more people, but they aren't sure how to attract new referrals.

Many therapists tell me it's easier for them to take a full sexual history from a client than to talk about their fee. Think about that for a moment.

My mission is to teach at least 10,000 therapists that you can make a good living helping people and it can be done in an ethical way that's a service to your clients and your community. I hope this book will help continue to "spread the word."

You will probably find this book different from other private practice marketing books, although it does include a lot of marketing suggestions.

This book is intended to get you thinking. I hope to challenge (in a good way) some of your beliefs about your practice, about money and about marketing. This is a coaching book and my goal is to inspire you to go deeper. As you read this book, you may find that new associations or ideas pop into your mind. I suggest you keep a journal nearby to jot down things that trigger you in some way. However, do not think that you need to implement all the ideas in this book. That would be "bingeing" and "bingeing" never works.

There are coaching questions for you at the end of each chapter. Consider reading this book with a colleague. For too long we have hidden the desire to make a profit in our practices. It's okay to discuss money. It's okay to want to earn a good, honest living. Let this book help initiate the conversation.

One final note: A major delight of mine is to share these points with graduate students. If you're affiliated with a graduate program, please contact me. Let's see how we can work together. I want the next generation of therapists to have the information that will prepare them to succeed should they chose a private practice career.

It takes courage to pick up a book like this. I am honored that you did so. Please let me know how it touches you.

Above all, I wish you great joy and success!

Love and blessings,

Casey

Foreword

We therapists have created a funny profession and developed one enormous contradiction.

We started with a dedication to helping other people create a more satisfying life. We invest an enormous amount of time, effort and expense to enrich the lives of our clients.

This is not a 9-5 occupation. In fact the "job" tends to dominate our lives even when not in the office.

There are many reasons why we choose this dedication. But making gobs of money was not one of them. In fact, for many of us, making money is simply a by product of doing good work. If our work is satisfying, that is where most of the rewards come from.

But then slowly another reality intrudes into Camelot. Something goes awry. The something has to do with the practical expense of living, saving and enjoying life beyond the simple pleasures.

Hoping to rise above the crass commercialism of many other professions (Wall Street, for example) we do our best to ignore the siren call of the mighty greenback. Alas, we get slapped back into the reality of everyday expenses and realizing even many small and simple pleasures extract their monetary toll.

We discover the collision between the values that pulled us into the profession and the human desire to improve our lot in life.

This collision between doing good and living well is not easily bridged by taking a graduate class in psychotherapy finances. It's like teaching the virtues of eating animal protein to vegetarians.

The same therapists who gladly and generously give economic discounts to clients who plead poor finances would never go to their neighborhood grocery store and ask for a reduction in their grocery bill because they cannot afford to pay for the items they want in their shopping cart. Nor would they try to negotiate a reduction in their utility bill on the grounds of needing to attend mandatory continuing education classes.

There are some therapists who will never read this book – even if given as a gift. For them, there is a kind of smugness in making a noble sacrifice for the sake of serving humanity. A subsistence level of living feels good –until they get ready to retire and realize travel means brown bagging it, staying at Motel 6, and driving their aging gas guzzling, bald tired vehicle they call a car.

That is when they will have wished they had read this book.

You have a treasure map in your hands. And like any treasure hunt you will have to invest to claim the bounty. You are in capable hands for this endeavor. Your guide is top notch in terms of knowledge, wisdom, and encouragement. She knows the terrain and where to lead you.

Listen to her and follow her advice until you gain your own confidence to build on what you have learned. Please don't stop growing after applying what you will learn from this marvelous book.

A wise person once told me that I could have more impact on people if it was ethically making a million dollars a year than someone in my profession who was earning $50,000 per year. That single comment had an enormous effect on my practice. I began to challenge my values that told me serving people and making money could not peacefully co-exist.

Please do not treat this book like many professional books we all read. We get the occasional insight and think that was worth the price of the book. Learning to make a difference and doing well are virtues that will have an impact on getting your clients to improve their lives as well.

As you grow economically so they will grow personally. We all win. It doesn't get any better than that. And that is what our profession is all about.

Good luck and good fortune in this vital area of your life.

Respectfully,

PETER PEARSON, Founder and Director, The Couples Institute

P.S. If I had a nickname for Casey, it would be "Allstate" – with her, you are in good hands.

When Casey asked me to write a forward for her book, I quickly said yes. Why? Because Casey is not a flake. I knew her ethics and that she would deliver value. Over the 2 years I have known Casey, I have watched her commitment to her clients and her own business. She can definitely help you "Make a Living While Making a Difference."

This book is a gem. It is full of practical strategies to successfully market your practice no matter what your personality type. She helps you understand that marketing professional services is about education, not about hype.

Learning from her and following her advice will be life changing. Years ago, I was a marketing-aversive therapist. I thought it was bad medicine. I have come to love the creativity involved in the process and the possibility to touch more people's lives.

I only wish there had been a Casey to guide me.

ELLYN BADER, Founder and Director, The Couples Institute

SECTION ONE

First Uncover the Myths

"Keep your thinking right and your
business will be right."
—Zig Ziglar

CHAPTER ONE

How It Happens To Most of Us

On a warm day in May 1989, I sat on Sandy's green, flowered couch and complained about my corporate job. Sandy had been my therapist for the last year. Her office was in a cute building in a sunny beach town in California. I really envied Sandy's schedule. She did three hours of therapy in the morning, took a long lunch and sometimes a nap. She then did three hours of therapy in the afternoon. This was her Monday through Thursday schedule. She took Fridays off.

Truth told, I had always thought that therapists had cool jobs. They were paid to help people. They could set their own schedules. They must hear the most fascinating stories. I had briefly considered becoming a therapist in the early 1980s, but was scared to leave my corporate job. I was a vice president at a major California bank earning a very good living.

I watched the trees sway in the breeze outside Sandy's window and confessed, "I have always wanted to be a therapist with a private practice, but I could never do it." A soft smile appeared on Sandy's face. I smiled back and it was like we both knew that, not only *could* I do it, I *would* do it.

Two weeks later I was enrolled in a graduate school on my way to my dream job.

Six years later, I opened the doors to my first private practice office.

Getting the office ready was so much fun. I was very concerned about privacy. I hired someone to install soundproofing drywall on the interior walls of the office. I had sound proofing material shot into the attic. I replaced the hollow core door to the office with a very heavy, solid core door. I made cafe curtains for the small window that faced the street.

The day my furniture came was very exciting. Here are two pieces of advice for those who haven't opened your doors yet:

1. Measure your office before you buy your furniture - half of my furniture had to be returned as it simply did not fit.

2. Sit in your furniture before you buy it. I am 5'1" tall and I bought a very large "therapist chair." It felt comfy in the show room. In my office however, I suddenly realized it was so big that my feet did not touch the floor. I looked like "Edith Ann", the mischievous five-year-old character created by comedienne Lily Tomlin, swinging her feet to and fro, in her oversized chair. Not the professional image I wanted to convey.

After making the necessary furniture adjustments, the office finally looked great, but I was not prepared at all for what happened next.

I could not get a client. Not one.

I did free talks at the church on a variety of topics. I went to therapist meetings and told them I was looking for clients. I advertised in the church bulletins, which cost me more per month than my rent and brought in a total of one client in six months. I hired a very expensive graphic artist who created beautiful business cards and letterhead that sat in my desk drawer.

The phone did not ring.

My dream of "three hours in the morning and three hours in the afternoon" was slipping away. Laid off from my day job at yet another psychiatric hospital, I decided to work on building my private practice full-time. But each month I went further and further into debt.

My friend Joe, a physician, had been lending me money to live on. I explained to him that I felt bad not repaying him and continuing to borrow money from him each month. He grinned and said, "Casey, I think of you as my retirement IRA."

That did it. I did not want to be anyone's IRA. I counted up my debts: $45,000. I counted up my income: $330 a month. Not good.

I made a plan. I sold my house and got a small apartment. I went back to my corporate roots and called upon my business training. I read everything I could on marketing. I hired a business coach.

There was another big hurdle to getting out of debt and making my practice financially viable - charging a fee. I was really scared of charging people. I had been told by a number of senior therapists that I could not make a good living being a therapist and so far they had been right. I was given well meaning, but ultimately bad advice about how to set fees. I was so uncomfortable talking about money with a potential client that I jumped to offer my lowest fee possible. Guilt hung over me like a cloud when I realized I was taking money just to help people. My money issues took a while to work through. This is not uncommon and we will talk much more about money and fees in the upcoming chapters.

In the beginning I made a lot of mistakes - ones I hope to keep you from making. But a few years later, I was out of debt with a full and fabulous practice.

To be honest, I feel a little let down by my therapist-training program. My teachers in graduate school had private practices, but no one taught me how to build one. No one explained what worked and what didn't. I was very well prepared to be a therapist, but totally ill equipped to be in the business of providing therapy.

That's why I am on this mission today. I want therapists to know how to build a great private practice. And I want them to know that they can make a good living doing it. We owe it to ourselves. We owe it to our clients. We owe it to the future of our profession.

In the early 2000's, I started teaching graduate students and newly licensed therapists how to set fees and how to build marketing plans that got them clients. These new private practitioners did so well, their supervisors called me asking what I was teaching. My friend Maria encouraged me - "No one is teaching these principles. We need to learn them. You need to teach this." That was the day my company, Be A Wealthy Therapist! was born.

WISDOM NUGGET:

Before you start thinking I am some money-hungry gold-digger, let me share my vision of 'Wealthy': I want to wake up, at least 6 days out of 7, happy to be me, happy to be in relationships with those I love and, happy to be doing work with clients I adore (and being paid well for it.)

This book is not about gouging clients.

It's about doing work you love and being paid well for it. It's about making an honest living while making a difference in people's lives. No need to reinvent the wheel. Let me share what has worked for me and for over 4,500 other therapists around the world.

Coaching Questions:

1. Did you start out in private practice or did circumstances influence you?

2. Did your graduate program prepare you for a career as a private practice business owner?

3. Before you read my definition, did you think "Wealthy Therapist" was an oxymoron? Do you still?

CHAPTER TWO

Your Field of Dreams

In the movie *Field of Dreams*, Ray Kinsella (played by Kevin Costner) is an Iowa corn farmer who is best described as a "dreamer." He keeps hearing a voice, "If you build it, he will come." Naturally, his family thinks he's delusional. Ray interprets this message as an instruction to build a baseball field on his farm. When he does, the ghosts of Shoeless Joe Jackson and the other seven Chicago White Sox players banned from the game for throwing the 1919 World Series appear and play ball.

"If you build it, they will come" is now a favorite movie quote for many of us. However, is it true in practice building? If we jump through all the licensing hoops and finally put out our shingle, will we have a thriving practice? If we build it, *will they come?*

WISDOM NUGGET

It used to be true that a private practitioner could have a full practice without ever marketing, but it's not true today.

In the past 40 years, there have been four significant eras for private practitioners.

1. The 1960's: During this time, a lot of people were in therapy. Often it was psychoanalysis. 'Self-growth' was a ruling value. We all wanted to "feel better." Most therapy was paid by indemnity insurance, which paid very well - usually 80% of the fee. This meant therapists earned a good living. Since people eagerly sought out therapy and it was not expensive for them, there was no need to create complex marketing plans. Almost all referrals came from word-of-mouth and many practitioners had very full practices.

2. The 1970's - early 1980's: The era of 'self-growth' continues, but many therapists didn't consider themselves businesspeople. Recently, I heard Dr. Nick Cummings say that as we came out of the Vietnam War era, business was something to be looked down upon. It was "bad" to be in business. Therapists could make a living helping people, but they didn't want to consider their practices a "business." Referrals still came from colleagues and clients. So, most therapists could still fill their practice without having to market. Besides, marketing was considered a business process and many (but of course not all) therapists saw themselves as private practitioners - not business people.

3. The Mid 1980's - the early 2000's: The cost of mental and behavioral healthcare is an area of concern for insurance companies as the amount they are paying providers increases. I have heard that during that time an alcoholic could get a year's stay in an inpatient facility paid for by his or her insurance company. Behavioral health companies were formed to "manage" the cost of mental health care. So, clients who had

been using their indemnity insurance now had to use managed care coverage to cover their therapy. In order to still see these clients, many therapists got on managed care panels. Reimbursement was lower so therapists had to see a lot more clients for less money and with more paperwork. During this time, therapy moved from a personal growth model to a medical model, in part, due to the advent of managed care in the US. Coupled with this, it became much less socially acceptable for people to be in therapy. To be in therapy, one had to have a "problem."

4. From 2000 - present: A new breed of therapist is coming out of graduate schools. Many are excited and looking forward to a private practice. No longer is business considered "bad." I lecture at campuses across the US and I see the change. These new therapists look forward to helping people and making a good living doing it. They are on fire about marketing and building their businesses. This is very good since it'll be very difficult for them to get on the already full managed care panels.

So, from the 1960's to the mid 1980's, it was true: if you hung out your shingle, the clients would fill your waiting room. It's no longer true. If you plan to have a private practice today and you do not already have a full caseload, you will be marketing your practice for the rest of your career.

Toward the end of *Field of Dreams*, the disgraced Chicago White Sox player, Shoeless Joe Jackson, arrives on the field built by Ray Kinsella. Shoeless Joe, clearly at home, asks Ray, "Is this Heaven?" Ray replies, "No, this is Iowa."

And your practice of today is not your professor's or your supervisor's private practice. However, you can be as successful as those before you. Perhaps even more if you wish. Ray followed his vision. I hope you do too.

There is great news. With some simple skills - and some maybe not-so-simple changes in your thinking - you can have the full and financially rewarding practice your really want. I have seen thousands of therapists do just that - therapists in tiny towns in rural areas and therapists in major metropolitan areas already saturated with private practitioners. It can be done.

1. Have you experienced other clinicians telling you, "I never had to market my practice and I always have a full caseload." After reading this chapter, can you see why that might be true?

2. Have you ever been discouraged when mentors have told you that they "did no marketing" yet they had a booming practice?

3. Who can you discuss these ideas with? A supervisor? A senior colleague? It would be interesting to hear about their history in terms of the eras of practice building.

SECTION TWO

Help Me Help You:

From Fear to Confidence to Wealthy: Yes You Can!

"Our deepest fear is *not* that we are inadequate. Our deepest fear is that we are *powerful* beyond measure. It is our light, not our darkness, that most frightens us.

We ask ourselves, who am I to be brilliant, gorgeous, talented, and fabulous? Actually, who are you not to be? You are a child of God. Your playing small doesn't serve the world."

—MARIANNE WILLIAMSON

CHAPTER THREE

Fear: Do I Deserve Success?

David Kuroda, LCSW, a licensed clinical social worker in Torrance, California was sharing his practice building strategies with me. David was the Division Chief in charge of Mediation at the Los Angeles County Superior Court before starting his practice in 2000. He had worked for the Courts for 18 years before venturing out on his own. Within three months of opening his practice, he was "in the black" and paying all of his expenses with his practice income. His practice has continued to grow over the years. He specializes in Mediation and Collaborative Divorce.

David says, "Whenever I talk to someone just starting a practice, my advice is to value yourself and your service. If you don't, why would anyone else?"

As of this writing, David routinely gets $300 an hour for mediation sessions. His therapy fee is $240 an hour. And he's busy.

David and I agree that in some ways, clinicians tend to be paid less than other professionals because we have not valued our contribution as much as other professionals. David noted, "As therapists, we tend to think that charging for our service is antithetical to giving the service. But by not charging an appropriate fee, we undervalue and undermine ourselves."

When David worked at the LA County Superior Court, he insisted that his staff was well compensated. This is because he knew that the work of his staff was at least as important as the District Attorneys who were putting criminals away. The mediators helped families avoid the adverse affects of divorce litigation. How can that be less important than the work of an attorney? To their credit, the Superior Court agreed.

Sarah R., a psychologist in NYC, routinely earns over $250,000 per year in her private practice and some years has made over $350,000. I asked Sarah how she's so successful. "I never thought that I was going to give away therapy. I know I make differences in people's lives. I have seen it. People have come in suicidal and leave a few years later doing great things with their lives with a deep knowing that they matter in this world. This is important, powerful work. I stay with people when they have lost hope and others have abandoned them. With great joy, I watch them move from desperate to purposeful. If I don't charge for that, I would be resentful and not at my best. How would that benefit anyone?"

Both Sarah and David care deeply about people and regularly give back to their communities. They give presentations and see some lower-fee clients. David put it well - "We don't want to be mercenaries. So to make sure this doesn't happen, I routinely do pro-bono work. For example, I see clergy and their families at no charge."

WISDOM NUGGET

The general public (as well as other professions) will not value us until we value ourselves. While it's important to give back to the community, it's also important not to devalue this work.

What makes Sarah and David different from other therapists?

1. *They understand their practice is a for-profit enterprise.*
2. *They recognize that they deserve to be paid well for the work they do.*
3. *They want the profession to flourish by making sure that our work is considered as valuable as our business counterparts. They know we need to start with ourselves.*

Coaching Questions:

1. Have your feelings about the profession changed since graduate school? If so, how?

2. Do you think that, as a profession, we don't value ourselves as much as other professions?

3. Would you recommend your daughter or son become a therapist? Why or why not?

Fear: What Will Happen if I Succeed?

In one of my weekend workshops, Larry sat low in his chair at the back of the room. While others shared their desire to grow their practice, Larry told the group, "I am only here for the continuing education units."

I asked the workshop participants, "What do you think keeps therapists making less than other health care professionals?"

Various important ideas were discussed. Jane said, "I believe we have done this to ourselves - by continuing to accept lower fees than our medical and legal counterparts, we perpetuate the idea that our work is not as valuable." That got some great discussion going.

Then I asked, "How do you feel about marketing your practice?" People groaned and shifted in their chairs. Then the follow up: "And how do you feel about making a good living from your practice?"

More groaning. People shared their discomfort:

"I can't stand the idea of marketing myself."

"Marketing is unprofessional."

"Marketing is just setting yourself up for more rejection."

"I tried marketing and I didn't get any new clients."

These are very common concerns. After working with thousands of therapists I've discovered two simple, yet surprisingly strong beliefs that can interfere with the private practitioner's desire for a financially successful practice. Most therapists seem to believe them to varying degrees. Here they are:

1. Money is bad.
2. Marketing is bad.

It's time to address those beliefs - and move past them.

1. Money is bad.

Money is not inherently bad. Yes, some people do bad things with money or in their attempts to get more money, but not everyone. Many people do very good things with money. Mother Teresa raised money all over the world for her causes.

Isn't it time to change how we think about money? Who does it serve to remain poor? My friend Chellie Campbell, author of *The Wealthy Spirit* and *From Zero to Zillionaire* says, "You can't help the poor and starving if you *are* the poor and starving." Let's put the oxygen mask on our face before we try and help others.

Think of money like a fine wine. Many can enjoy it. Some people will abuse it. But it's not the wine itself that's bad.

2. Marketing is bad.

If you have watched any daytime TV lately and seen all those cheesy commercials for personal injury attorneys, you may think so. But again, it's like the wine.

If you do not market your practice, fewer people will know you're there to help them. If you want to help more people you need to let more people know how to find you. Marketing is not some slick attempt to make money. Marketing is simply the way to let more people know you're there to help, and it can be done with honor.

I don't expect that these simple thoughts will "do it" for you. Don't worry. We will be tackling them in much more detail in the next two sections.

When I handed Larry his CEU certificate at the end of the workshop, he smiled and said: "Before this weekend, I didn't really think I could have a practice with fee-for-service clients without sacrificing my soul. I did not want to be a rich, arrogant clinician who makes decisions that are in my interest, but not in my client's best interest. But I get it now. I can increase my income and I owe that to my family. And I can do it in an honorable way that serves my family, the client and my community."

Go, Larry!

WISDOM NUGGET

Be true to yourself. It takes courage to look at what limiting beliefs you may have about your practice. Consider sharing this with a trusted confidant. Let them challenge you. You will become clearer on what is true for you.

Money and Marketing are not bad words. But we have been brainwashed into thinking they are. It is time to move past those beliefs. Take back your power now. Remember the wine.

You can ethically market your practice and make an honest living in ways that serve everyone.

Coaching Questions:

1. On a scale of 1 - 10 (with 1 being 'very true' and 10 being 'very false') how true for you is the statement - "Money is bad"?

2. Rate your comfort with the idea of marketing your practice on a scale of 1 - 10 (with 1 being 'very uncomfortable' and 10 being 'very comfortable').

3. Now, consider your commitment to your practice. How committed are you to building your practice?

4. What beliefs do you have that might get in the way of building the practice you really want?

Fear: There Won't Be Enough Money for Me

Have you ever thought about those expressions? *Dirt poor. Filthy rich.* It seems that money is dirty - regardless of whether you have money or you don't. I was curious, so I looked up the origins of these expressions. They appear to have come out of the 15th and 16th centuries.

Dirt poor is thought to come from the fact that only wealthy families used to have planks as floorboards in their homes. The poor people had no wooden floor planks - just actual dirt floors in their homes.

Filthy rich is interpreted by many as, "very rich - and they probably became so in a dishonorable way." In the 14th century, the word "lucre" meant money. References to "lucre" were often negative giving rise to the expressions "foul lucre" or "filthy lucre." In the 1920's, this became an expression in American slang - "filthy rich."

Yet, what is money actually? Is it dirty? Well, maybe it is. The Miami Herald conducted a study in 1985, which asked 11 prominent local citizens to supply a $20 bill for testing, including the Catholic archbishop, the first President George Bush's son Jeb, and Janet Reno. 10 out of the 11 bills had traces of cocaine. But I digress...

Is money the root of all evil? Or is it simply a medium of exchange in transactions?

Money is currency. It's not good or bad. Greed is bad, but we are not talking about greed. We are talking about being paid for your service.

But what does it mean when you take money from your client as payment for your services? It means that you have money to put back into the economy. Perhaps you have a client that works for a grocery store. After she pays you, you go to the grocery store and buy groceries. Your client's employer now has more money; they can continue to stay in business and pay your client her salary.

This is a little simplistic, but I hope you can see where I am going with this. Not only does your client get great therapy, she continues to get paid by her employer because of your purchases.

Of course, economics is not this simple and there are usually many steps in between. You may shop at a rival grocery store. But their employees may spend money at your client's family business. Money is constantly in motion and this makes the economy strong.

I bring this up because many people feel that taking money from a client (read: charging a fee) means that the client will have less money. Maybe initially this is true. But if the economy works, as it should, your client will continue to have the money that's hers.

Also, with your income you pay taxes. Your tax dollars go to fund programs for the poor. You're still serving the poor when you're earning a good living.

Think of the other clichés and sentiments we grew up with: Money doesn't grow on trees. Save for a rainy day. There is never enough money. Rich people are bad. It's easier to marry a rich man than a poor one. It's easier for a camel to get through the eye of a needle than for a rich man to get into the kingdom of God. (Since it said "rich man" I assumed I was exempt from this one.)

Let me tell you about Alison, a therapist in Dallas, Texas. She's smart, vivacious and a strong introvert. She came to me to help her build a marketing plan to attract more fee-for-service clients. Yet, I quickly discovered that Alison had a lot of limiting beliefs about money and earning a good living.

Alison had been raised in sheer opulence. Her father was a very prominent lawyer. They had butlers and nannies and gold-trimmed fine china. But when Alison wanted candy money, she was told there wasn't enough money.

Alison was sent to boarding school in ninth grade and while the other students had spending money, she had just enough to pay for the necessities. She grew up with an internal script, "Other people are entitled to money, but I am not. There is never enough money for *me*."

After college, Alison worked in low-paying jobs. She lived very frugally but was always strapped for cash. She earned a masters degree in counseling and tried to start a private practice, but never made enough to pay the rent. Yet she felt a calling to help people. Somewhere inside Alison, she felt she should be able to make enough money to at least pay her bills. She wanted there to be enough money for *her*.

Alison and I worked together for six months. While she came to me to help her build a marketing plan, I knew right away that would be a bad place to start. I have done this work long enough to know that the number one predictor of a financially successful therapist in private practice is how they feel about money.

We never got to the marketing plan. We focused on her beliefs. Once Alison's beliefs towards money changed, she realized that her practice was changing too. Her phone rang more often. Clients didn't leave treatment early. Finally, I asked Alison to tally her income. She was shocked when she discovered that her private practice income had increased by $20,000 over the six months we worked together - that was a 33% increase without doing any additional marketing. By simply working on those old worn out beliefs that didn't serve her anymore, she made an additional $20,000 in six months. She has gone on to make a lot more since then. It brings a warm smile to my heart every time I think about Alison and her success.

You deserve to make a good living. In fact, I know that you're worth your weight in gold. How's that for a great money cliché?

WISDOM NUGGET

The more money you earn, the more money you will have "to save, to share and to spare."

The number one predictor of a financially successful therapist in private practice is how they feel about money.

Check your beliefs about money. Are they hindering you from getting the practice you really want?

Remember, money is neither good nor bad - it's simply a medium of exchange.

Coaching Questions:

1. When you think about having more money, how do you feel?

2. What would it say about you if you had all the money you wanted?

3. How would your life change if you had all the money you wanted?

Fear: But Everyone Wants to Use Insurance

I was so excited. I had just removed myself from my last insurance panel. I was free. I couldn't wait for the 'fee-for-service' clients to be knocking down my door.

My marketing efforts were working because my phone was ringing. However, call after call I was asked, "Do you take insurance?" While I was so excited about not taking insurance, potential clients were really disappointed that I didn't.

How did I respond when they asked about insurance? First, I'd gulp. Then say, "No, sorry." The potential client would thank me, hang up and move on to someone who did.

Then I remembered Nancy and her new prescription sunglasses. Nancy had been my business coach. She wore prescription eyeglasses but had never purchased prescription sunglasses. After all, she would have to purchase two pair of glasses every time her prescription changed and who wants to do that? So she didn't wear sunglasses.She was driving (without sunglasses of course) one day and an ad for an eyeglass store came on the radio: "Do you know that you're burning your retina each day you do not wear sunglasses? Reduce your chances of developing several eye diseases by wearing sunglasses. Order your sunglasses today and stop burning your eyes!"

Nancy drove immediately to the eyeglass store and ordered a pair of sunglasses. The moral of the story is, sometimes we don't know what we need unless it's explained to us.

People with health care coverage will often want to use their insurance to pay for all or a part of their therapy. This is natural. Most doctors will bill insurance companies for their patient's treatment. So expect that potential clients will ask you if you take insurance.

Of course if you have signed a contract with their insurance company agreeing to accept patients for a fixed fee, then you must honor your contract. But, if you haven't, don't assume that because a potential client asks you about insurance it means they are stuck on the idea of using it. Please don't take the insurance question as a negative. It's a request for information. It might also be an opportunity – let me explain.

After several of these calls from prospective clients that ended with "No, sorry." I began to ask myself what were the real reasons I did not want to take third-party payments. Of course I wanted to be in charge of my income and my caseload. Of course I was tired of the lower fees and all that paperwork. But there were other reasons too. Number one was the fundamental reason regarding the privacy and sacredness of the confidential therapeutic relationship. Maybe it was time to tell prospective clients what it meant when we did bill their insurance.

So the next time I was asked that question, I thought about my reasons and my commitment to the client's confidentiality. The conversation started with me saying something like this:

"You know, last year my husband had surgery and he needed an MRI beforehand. I was so grateful to have insurance to cover those expenses. But, I personally don't like to bill insurance companies for the therapy I provide. May I tell you why?"

I didn't want to force my reasons on anyone else. I wanted to make sure that the prospect wanted to know my line of thinking about insurance. If he or she really wanted to use their insurance and didn't care why I didn't take it, then there was no sense prolonging the conversation. So first I validated their desire to use insurance and then I asked, "May I tell you why?" in a very respectful tone. I did not continue until I had an affirmative response. It turned out that over 80% of people really did want to know why.

For those 80% who were interested I would explain, "There are several reasons I don't like to bill insurance companies for therapy. First, in order to have your insurance pay for your therapy, I have to give you (I'd say this next part, very s-l-o-w-l-y) a mental disorder diagnosis. I really don't want to give anyone a (again, slowly) mental disorder diagnosis. That's just not the way I like to work. Then, depending on the insurance company, I may have to write a report every five to ten sessions to show that you're still sick with that mental disorder. For them to continue paying for therapy, my report needs to show that you're still sick and getting better, but that you aren't cured yet. I really don't want to write a report like that – sharing the details of your mental disorder."

This usually got their attention, and I'd continue: "Then someone from the insurance company who doesn't know either of us is going to read that report and assess how well our work is going and decide if they will continue to pay for the therapy. It's like they are sitting in the room judging us and how we are doing. Of course no one from the insurance company really is in the room with us, but it can feel like they are. I don't know about you, but I think how well the therapy is going should be something that you and I decide - not someone who doesn't know either of us."

As the conversation continued, I'd share more information, "I don't know if this is true or not, but I have heard that up to 14 people at the insurance company could potentially read that report before they'd agree to pay for continuing therapy. Again - I am not sure if that's true, but I just don't feel comfortable with that possibility. Also, if you're self-employed or ever might be, a mental disorder diagnosis on your record can make getting health care insurance very expensive. That's why I don't take insurance. However, as I said, I totally understand your desire to use it. So, here are a couple of options: Either you can go back to your insurance carrier and get another referral or, I have openings Wednesday at noon or Thursday at four. What do you think you'd like to do?"

Then I was quiet, giving them time to process all that information.

Fifty percent of the people hearing that script became my fee-for-service clients. We went on to do great work together. Many referred their friends and explained to them that I did not take insurance and the reasons why.

I have been accused of being manipulative with this script. I guess you could look at it that way, but I really believe the prospective client needs to understand the impact of using insurance. Then he or she can make an informed decision. The benefits of using insurance are clear. The risks usually aren't. By sharing these reasons, we have told the truth. The client can then weigh the risks and benefits and make their own decision.

WISDOM NUGGET

Just as it was Nancy's choice to buy sunglasses or not, your clients can choose to see you for therapy and have their records remain private or, they can choose to use their insurance. The choice is theirs. Don't be afraid to share the truth. My hunch is, if you do, your appointment book will fill up faster than if you just say "No, sorry. I don't take insurance."

---

1. *If you are a contracted provider, make sure you understand your contract. Please don't tell prospective clients you don't take insurance if you have agreed to do so.*
2. *If you do not take insurance, create your own script to use when you're asked, "Do you take insurance?"*
3. *Be gracious if the client wants to use insurance rather than paying you "out of pocket." We all want to use our insurance at times.*

Coaching Questions:

1. Do you use insurance personally? If so, for what types of services?

2. What is your emotional reaction to this chapter? Was there a knot in your stomach as you read it? Did you find a sense of relief at all?

3. What (if anything) will you do differently as a result of reading this chapter?

CHAPTER SEVEN

Confidence: There Will Be Enough Chocolate Cake

Here is a question I get almost daily.

"Casey, how do I let go of these old beliefs and start believing it's okay to make a good living?"

Several years ago, my coach asked me over the phone to notice how often I thought in terms of "not having enough." I couldn't imagine that I thought that way and denied I did. She encouraged me to "just notice" if, and when it occurred. I agreed to the exercise in a rather dismissive fashion.

After I hung up, I grabbed my purse to go to my favorite soup and salad restaurant. This was one of those "salad-buffet" restaurants where you pick up a plate when you enter, fill it with lots of salad, and then pay for your lunch before sitting. Then people can get their choice of soups, pastas, and desserts from other parts of the restaurant. I love this place.

As I drove up, I realized there were no parking spaces. Grumbling, I went up and down a few rows before I found one. Then I went into the restaurant, got in the line with my plate, and started to fill it with salad.

It was busy that day and there were many people ahead of me waiting to pay for their lunch. My eyes searched the dessert table.

There was one piece of chocolate cake left. Just one. I started to freak out. Would I get there in time? My heart started to race. I willed the people in front of me to move faster.

After I paid for my food, I raced over to the dessert table and snatched that lonely piece of cake. I couldn't believe that my hands were actually shaking. I was really afraid I wouldn't get any cake.

I sat down - still shaking - and started to have a talk with myself. First, I was congratulating myself on the smooth moves I made to get to the cake before anyone else did. (When you're only 5' 1" you can sneak in between the tall people.) Then I wondered if someone needed to do an intervention with me - this much worry over a piece of cake?

I looked around the restaurant trying to calm down. Then I saw it.

A server was bringing out an entire cookie sheet full of new, warm chocolate cake.

I stabbed the piece I had with my fork. It was dry and a bit hard.

Then I just started giggling. "Me?" I thought to myself. "Worried about not having enough?" It had been less than 30 minutes from my coach's challenge and I was in the throws of "lack" thinking.

If you want to make peace with money, start by looking at your beliefs and challenge them as we've talk about.

When I coach therapists to build their practices, we always start with the money and their feelings about it. No matter how great the marketing plan, if we haven't decided we are worthy of a good living and have good skills with setting, negotiating and collecting the fee, we won't attract the income we say we want.

There are more than enough clients for all the clinicians in private practice - no matter how saturated your area is with therapists. There is enough money to go around.

Now you can have your cake and eat it too.

By the way, I did get a piece of the fresh, warm cake that day. In fact I ate both pieces.

WISDOM NUGGET

If you think there aren't enough clients or that you will never make a good living, then you will be right. Consider that, just maybe, there are enough clients and there are clients who will be willing to pay your full fee.

Coaching Questions:

1. Ask yourself how your old beliefs about money serve you now. Review your family of origin issues about money and worth. Do you believe that you're worthy of a good wage? If not, review how your family of origin might have impacted your beliefs. Then do whatever interventions you need to do (cognitive restructuring, EMDR or TFT or EFT) with yourself to change those beliefs. Spend some time with yourself on these old beliefs about money and your income will increase. It happens every time.

2. Take a page from the coaching assignment I was given - notice how often your thoughts are focused on "not having enough." It's only when we come out of that denial can we really set the stage to have what we want.

Confidence: Therapists as Surgeons

Therapists have incredible hearts of gold. Seriously. Who else could listen to people talk about their pain several hours a day, week after week? We hear about so much sadness: death, divorce, illness, trauma, abuse, exhaustion from taking care of an aging relatives and joblessness. Of course there are the wonderful aspects too, which is why we do this work. The joys of seeing a wayward teen do well in college. The sheer relief we feel when a woman in a very abusive relationship finally leaves and finds that she can sleep through the night without fear. The pleasure at seeing a couple on the brink of divorce, find that spark again.

I don't have to tell you that being a therapist is an honor and a huge responsibility. At the end of each day you don't "leave everything at the office" the way other professionals might be able to do. As a therapist, you hold your clients in your mind and in your heart even when you aren't in the room with them. How often do you talk with colleagues about a particularly challenging case? How often do you attend specific CEU programs because you're searching for ways to help one special client? How many times does a song on the car radio remind you of a client?

You don't do therapy – you are a therapist. You help people. Not only with timely therapeutic interventions, but also just by being you - with your heart and your desire to enter deeply into the therapeutic relationship with a client. You help them just by being in the room with them, listening to them and caring about them.

Your smile or your wistful look, or even the proverbial "kick in the rear" helps people move from being unhappy with their lives to feeling that life is bearable. You help people move from feeling worthless to believing in themselves.

WISDOM NUGGET

You can honestly, ethically help people and still make a good living.

You're doing such important work.

Whether a patient is suffering from a broken heart or is experiencing a cardiac problem, the patient's healthcare provide deserves to be paid well to help that person back to optimal health.

Your work is no less important than a physician's work.

Coaching Questions:

1. Doing therapy for many clinicians is as natural to them as drinking a glass of water. Is it easy for you to see the incredible value you provide to your clients or do you tend to downplay it?

2. What do you think about the idea that you're as valuable as a surgeon?

3. Are you, or do you know of, a clinician who rarely questions his or her value or worth? What is the internal self-talk that makes that confidence possible?

CHAPTER NINE

Wealthy: Yes You Can!

I sat nervously across from three men in expensive suits. They were from a large corporation and were visiting my undergraduate campus recruiting entry-level computer programmers. I was 21 years old and about to graduate with a bachelor's degree in computer science. They had been asking me questions for almost an hour: about computers, my strengths and weaknesses and my willingness to move to another state. I was getting really tired, but I wanted to impress upon them what a great hire I would be.

I had prepared extensively for this interview. I rehearsed some great answers to potential questions and I was ready. When asked my greatest regret, I did not share some unprocessed, deep dark secret that would have them calling the psychiatric evaluation team. Instead I paused and then mused wistfully, "I wish I had been a better gymnast and gone to the State competition with my high school gymnastics team." I was on a roll.

One of them asked, "And what would your salary requirements be?"

"Oh, it doesn't matter." I said. "I am sure whatever you'd offer would be fair and fine."

One man's head popped up. The other two looked startled. I took that to mean they liked me. Heck, I was willing to come cheap!

That night I phoned my businessman dad. He loved my answer about my deepest regret and some of the other responses I had given.

"Did they talk to you about the salary?" he asked.

"Oh, I told them the money didn't matter." I replied.

Luckily this conversation was over the phone. I could imagine my dad rolling his eyes. Right then and there he gave me some important lessons about money.

He told me that, right or wrong, people would judge us by money. "Casey, if you don't ask for a good salary, they will assume you don't value your contribution very much. They won't see you as a strong person who cares about herself. They want to hire people who value themselves."

I didn't get an offer from the three men in suits. But I learned my lesson. I did get 10 job offers from the next 10 interviews I did. And with the one I accepted, I even negotiated a higher entry-level salary than my friends who had been working in the field for three years were earning. It was fun.

Years later, I left the corporate world to become a therapist and help people and I forgot the lessons my dad had taught me.

How did I forget?

As a trainee acquiring supervised hours toward licensure, I was required to work in a non-profit agency or in a hospital. I did both. In both the psych hospitals and the non-profit agencies, I served the poorest of the poor. These people were either homeless or on some type of public assistance and most of them had severe mental disorders. Keeping a job was not usually an option for these folks. I began to think that most people just could not afford therapy.

When I left the agencies and went into private practice, I took this belief with me. No longer was I looking at the "three hours in the morning and three hours in the afternoon" with more than enough money to pay my bills. I was looking at hours and hours of work with very sad cases for very low fees just to make ends meet. The thought of charging a higher fee (even $50) was scary enough to send me for refuge with Ben and Jerry's Chocolate Chip Cookie Dough Ice Cream - except I couldn't afford it! I was miserable.

Then a colleague told me a story about a wealthy woman who wouldn't get inpatient alcohol treatment. The state-sponsored treatment facilities were old, worn out places filled with people with dual diagnoses and, often, severe mental disorders. While it may seem politically incorrect, she said she would go into treatment if the therapist could find her a "more comfortable" place. The therapist recommended a treatment facility that cost $10,000 a month. The client went in and has been sober ever since.

It's noble to care about the poor and to make sure there is adequate mental health care available to them and, in many states, it's easy for low-income families to get free or low-cost therapy. Then something occurred to me. Who is inviting the wealthier people to get help? Who is telling them that we understand they have problems too?

That was the day I decided not to discriminate against the wealthy people. Wealthy people can use help too. I wanted to be there to offer it to them. I've heard that theologian and counselor Eugene Kennedy once said that he would rather have a rich client than a poor client because the rich client knew that money didn't solve all problems.

Don't get me wrong. Some of my caseload has been pro-bono work. I spent nine years working in hospitals with geriatric psychiatric patients and with chronically and severely mentally ill adults. I have been whacked in the face with a full adult diaper and stabbed by a fork. I have stayed with paranoid naked adults huddled on their hospital bathroom floor. I have always had a great love and desire to help these people.

It took me quite a while to accept the fact that it's okay to charge a good fee to people in my private practice. I felt I owed it to everyone to offer the lowest possible fee. What I discovered was - just like those men who interviewed me at college - many people want to feel that you're offering them something valuable.

After accepting this truth the most amazing thing happened.

Once I began to value myself and charge a higher fee, my caseload grew. People had more confidence in me. And my confidence grew.

As my dad had said, "like it or not, money matters." If you're called to poverty, embrace it and enjoy it. If not, please value yourself and value the important work that you do. And let others know you value it too.

WISDOM NUGGET

Make sure you have a clear strategy for setting up your fees. Know that if you always offer the lowest possible fee or, if you lower your fee regularly, you may be thought of as one who doesn't value their contributions.

Coaching Questions:

1. What did you learn about money growing up that affects your earning potential today?

2. Do you feel called to embrace poverty? Or, are you trying to figure out how you might earn more?

3. Is there a colleague or friend that you might discuss some of these ideas with?

SECTION THREE

Be Wealthy:

The 7 Point Overview

"Money is better than poverty,
if only for financial reasons."
—WOODY ALLEN

#1: Dream:
But I Just Want to Have a Nice Practice

People often ask me if they need a business plan to start their practice. If you want to create one, there are some great resources. The small business administration provides assistance. There are zillions of books on the subject. I personally like *The One Page Business Plan* by Jim Horan.

This is probably considered blasphemy by other business coaches, but I don't think you need a big-deal business plan. In my experience, struggling for weeks over a business plan is one way to postpone getting started with your practice.

So what *do* you need to get started?

Remember, as a therapist in private practice, you're a business owner. As such, you need to know what you want that business to look like. I call this "The Vision." You need to know when and where you want to see clients.

You need to know what your "office hours" will be and you need to know how much money you want your business to bring in each year. You need to know whom you serve and what products and services you will offer them. You need to know how you plan to get the word out about your services. (This is your marketing plan - you do need a marketing plan.)

Grab a pen and daydream a bit. Make a list of all the things that you really do not want in your practice. This can include the type of client or specific diagnoses. You may not want to see children or narcissistic men. You may not want to work evenings or weekends.

It may be something related to your office location or suite-mates. You may not want to share office space with anyone that wears perfume, for example. For me, this is especially important as I blow up like a blowfish when I'm near some scents. In the first office I shared with others, my eyes watered so hard due to residual cologne on the therapist's chair, my clients were offering *me* the tissue box.

You may not want to do a lot of insurance company paperwork. You may not want to see more than 10 clients a week - or you may not want to see less than 30. You may not want to be the only one that answers your phone. It doesn't matter how big or how small - just get it all out. Please write at least 30 things you do not want in your practice. It's better if you can come up with 50. You may want to spend a week doing this assignment. Don't let it slide. Only when you know what you *don't* want, can you put together a practice you really *do* want. For example, I knew I did not want to see alcoholics, do child custody evaluations or ever testify in court. When referrals came in requesting any of the above services, I was very clear that I didn't want to do that type of work. My standard response was "You know, I am just not good at that. I really want you to work with someone who is good at that. May I offer you some referrals?" By the way, this is a great line to use with borderline personality disordered referrals. They want (and deserve) someone who has the love and patience for that type of work.

I remember one time a woman insisted on "interviewing" me as well as other therapists. Today I would encourage someone who was "interviewing" therapists to go ahead and interview all the other therapists first. If he or she had not found a good match after seeing others, then I would be happy to meet with them. When a therapist knows they are being interviewed, it creates an odd shift in the energy. It's easy to get pulled into wanting to please the potential client in order to be the one "chosen." This can be avoided if the client has found the other therapists interviewed did not suit him or her.

However, a warning here:

If a potential client interviews several other therapists and doesn't find one that fits his or her needs, it's probably a safe bet that sooner or later you won't either. I heard Carl Whitaker tell a story once that a woman came to see him and said, "You will be my eighth therapist." Dr. Whitaker suggested she take all the money she would have spent on therapy with him and go to a cabin in the woods for a few months. He did not want to be the "eighth therapist who failed." Apparently she followed his advice and months later came back and reported that she felt great.

Back to the list. Now that you have a long list of what you don't want, take each item and turn it into a positive statement on a new list. This will be the list of what you *do* want. Start each sentence with "I look forward to..." or, "I love it that..." or, "I am excited to see..." or, "It's fun to..." and, "More and more I am..."

My friend Debbie has been a therapist for seven years. She has only recently decided to actively market for fee-for-service clients and remove herself from insurance company panels. She volunteered her list for you to see:

1. I love it that I choose to have only fee-for-service clients in my practice.
2. More and more I am accepting full-fee clients.
3. I look forward to having my appointment book full with motivated couples.
4. I am excited to see that many couples are able and want to come in for therapy during the daytime.
5. It is fun to see my emergency and irregular expenses funds growing.
6. I love letting others see how much I enjoy helping couples get along better.
7. More and more I realize that I offer a great service and speak about my fee easily.

8. I love seeing myself make $5,000 and more each month.

9. I've decided to honor myself by keeping my "office hours."

10. More and more I am comfortable with marketing my practice.

11. I love surrounding myself with colleagues who understand the business of psychotherapy. Debbie loved this exercise and decided to apply it to the rest of her life as well.

12. I've decided to make sleep a priority.

13. It is fun to eat food that agrees with me.

14. I've decided to get good exercise.

15. I love how it feels when I take good care of myself.

Debbie told me she reads her list daily and it propels her make good decisions about her clients, her money and her time off.

Once you make your list of what you *do* want within your practice, it's time to look for limiting beliefs. Let's say that you have on your list, "I love to see myself make $5,000 a month." (Or $10,000 or $15,000 - whatever your goal.) How does it feel when you say that? Do you freak out a little? A lot? What do you say to yourself? Do you say, "I could never do that"? If so, it may be time for a reality check. Have others ever made that much money? Why could they do it and you can't? Then just maybe you can say to yourself, "Just today, hundreds of therapists in my state (maybe even thousands) have made that much per month. Why can't I do it too?"

WISDOM NUGGET

Studies have shown that, people who write down their goals achieve them more often than those who don't.

---

*I recommend you develop a
vision as opposed to a huge
business plan.*

*See yourself in that vision.
Delight in what it feels and
looks like.*

Savor it.

*Know what you don't want and
what you do want.*

So, what is your vision?

Coaching Questions:

1. Are you intrigued enough to do this assignment?

2. Will you actually create the list of 30 or more items that you don't want and then list what you do want? Or are you likely to skip this?

3. Is there a colleague, friend of family member who can share your excitement about your vision?

CHAPTER ELEVEN

#2: Believe:
Do You Have a Business Or a Hobby?

Twenty-five of us from all walks of entrepreneurship were at our local chapter meeting of Women's Referral Service. We had networked, finished our chicken taco salad and now it was time for the speaker. As I savored the last bite of my raspberry cheesecake the lunchtime speaker began.

She was a financial planner. She was a lovely, soft-spoken, intelligent woman who discussed SEP-IRAs, trusts, annuities and other types of investing. She reminded us how much money we would need in order to retire (the dreaded "number.") She spoke in very simple terms and I learned a lot that day about tracking my income, expenses and investments.

As she ended her talk, she paused dramatically, making eye contact with many of us in the room, and spoke:

"I know there are a lot of 'solo-preneurs' here - people who have a sole proprietorship company. It can be wonderful and lonely to work alone. It's easy to forget that you must work on your business and not just in your business. So make sure you market your business and track your money. Make a profit. Because, if you don't make a profit then you have a hobby, not a business."

You could have heard a pin drop. Every single one of us was staring at her and I think some of us had stopped breathing. My business life started to flash before my eyes. My goals were simple: 1) help people 2) pay my bills. That was it. If I did that, I was happy.

Having a business was something I wanted to avoid. I had done the corporate and management 'thing'. I was tired of skirted suits and high heels. I knew I just wanted to have people sit on my couch for 45 minutes and leave after I provided them with brilliant therapeutic interventions. I did not want the stress and headaches of managing office personnel or other corporate responsibilities.

Then I had another thought. I had no money saved for retirement. I had not taken an actual vacation in six years. When my car needed major repairs, I had to charge it on a credit card since I didn't have any emergency funds. My clothes often came from the discount store – and, truth be told - sometimes from second-hand shops. I was terrified my computer would crash because - although I had been meaning to - I had not saved a cent for the new one I knew I'd need soon. Somehow, I was always surprised when my annual car insurance bill showed up.

My dad's visit that weekend was serendipitous. He's a great support of my business venture. He asked, "So, you making any money at this therapist business?" Good heavens. I had no idea how to answer that question. I had gone over my figures after listening to the financial planner earlier that week and realized I was breaking even (if I didn't count the emergency charges on my credit card, zero savings, and dining on 99 cent green burritos at the local taco place most nights.) It was time to make a change.

The first thing I did was look at my aversion to actually having a business. I was comparing my tiny therapy practice to a billion dollar corporation. It seemed there had been only two options in my mind - breaking even or, managing a huge corporation with the associate worries about buildings, equipment, customers, suppliers and employees. To think those were the only two options open to a business owner was ridiculous.

I began to design a financial plan for the practice I wanted. Instead of ignoring the fact that I hadn't taken a vacation, I put a category for one into the budget. I created an "emergency fund" for unexpected expenses such as broken water heaters. An "irregular expense account" was created to save (in advance) for expenses that came throughout the year - for example, malpractice insurance and continuing education classes.

Wisdom Nugget

Many therapists start their practices as part-time ventures and therefore don't consider them "businesses."

As you can imagine, I needed to bring in more money than I had been earning. Some changes needed to be made in the way I ran my practice in order to have the additional money. Later in the book, we will talk about how to calculate how much money you need. We will also discuss ways that you can bring in that additional money.

In all honesty, it took a couple of years to really get the hang of being on top of my money. I remember one October I made more money than I had made in the prior two months put together. It was very exciting. I made a huge contribution to my SEP-IRA. I bought a gorgeous designer purse. I all but stopped my marketing efforts as I basked in all that money. November came and went. Then December hit. It seemed that every client I had decided to take a break during the month of December. I had no money saved for the seasonal lulls in my practice. That became a new category in my financial plan and the next year I took off three weeks in December. The "December Money" was already in the bank and I enjoyed my vacation.

Little by little, my income increased and my retirement account grew. Going out for a nice lunch with a girlfriend was a treat rather than a worry. For the first time in my private practice career I started to relax. I had a business with a well-planned safety net.

Some of the therapists that I coach readily admit they want to practice therapy as a hobby. They would like their practice income to compensate them for their practice expenses, but these practitioners have no need for their private practice income to pay for any personal or household expenses. Usually these are clinicians who already have a lot of money or they have a family member who is supporting their household expenses, "Not that there is anything wrong with that" – to borrow a phrase from Jerry Seinfeld. We all have hobbies and if providing therapy is yours, more power to you.

My concern is with the thousands of clinicians who have not felt it was okay to make a profit - the ones who haven't looked at their numbers out of fear or ignorance and are worrying about paying the rent at the end of each month. It doesn't have to be that way. You can learn a few new skills or implement some you already know and start enjoying a lifestyle with less worry and more fun and freedom.

Somewhere along the way, many of us got the impression that owning and operating a "for-profit" psychotherapy business was shameful. But would we ever think that about another small business? We applaud small business owners every day. We enjoy visiting and supporting the independent bookshop, the community hardware store and the local diner. Celebrate your entrepreneurship!

Coaching Questions:

1. Is yours a business or a hobby? Which would you like it to be?

2. How do you provide for your irregular and emergency expenses?

3. With which colleagues can you open a discussion about the business of therapy?

#3: Market:
Where Do I Find the Clients That Want to Pay Me $150?

Someone in the Exclusive Members Program asked me a great question: "Where are the $150/hour clients?" This chapter is my response to that question.

Many therapists wonder how in the world they are going to find a caseload of people who want to pay them their full fee. These clinicians do great work, yet not enough people walk through their doors. Many want to know how to do less managed care work and have more clients that can afford to pay them a good fee.

We don't find these clients by looking for people who have extra money. We begin at the beginning. What problem do you help to solve and who wants to pay you to help them solve it?

If you help parents who are worried that their teen is on the wrong path, you will have potential clients. If you market this service by building relationships with referral sources and prospects in wealthier areas, you will have cash-paying clients.

If you have a problem and find someone you know can help, is how much money they charge always your biggest concern? I have hired coaches, therapists, and attorneys because I thought they could help me. If they charged $25 or $50 more per hour than someone else, it wasn't an issue. I believed the person could help me with my problem now. I liked them. I was ready. I hired them.

In my workshops, I often ask people if they "shopped" dentists for the best price when they had a root canal problem. Of the hundreds I posed this question to, only one did. We just want to be out of pain. It goes back to this: if I believe you have the solution to my problem and I like you and trust you, I will hire you.

WISDOM NUGGET

There is an interesting phenomenon that happens around fee-setting. Once you decide you are confident with the fee you are charging, your prospective clients will more readily accept as well.

Having said that, demographics do play an important role in marketing. If I am marketing my services to parents of teens in a poor area of town, I will probably find fewer $150 clients than if I market in a wealthier area. Notice what type of pond you're fishing in.

I've had many therapists tell me that no one wants to pay full fee and competition among therapists is high. I guess I have been lucky in that my mentors never thought this way. In fact, all eight therapists in our suite have full practices and I think only one takes insurance.

So, get the word out. As my friend Chellie says, "You want clients who pay you and praise you." You deserve this.

Your $150 clients are nearby.

They just need to know what problem you can help them with.

They need to trust you with that problem.

Finally, they need to be in enough pain to want to pay someone to help them with their problem.

Coaching Questions:

1. Have you found yourself wondering about how to find people to pay your full fee?

2. What are the limiting beliefs preventing you from attracting them - such as "no one will pay out-of-pocket?"

3. What benefits can you imagine would be yours if you decided to approach marketing therapy in the ways we are discussing in this book?

#4: Ask:
A Penny (or maybe $150)
For Your Thoughts

You can probably relate to my coaching client, Laura. No one in her graduate psychology program talked about fees - setting, negotiating or collecting them. That was left to her internship. She worked at several low-cost non-profit agencies during her internship that offered very low-cost counseling to the poor. She was lucky enough to work in one agency where she learned some excellent money skills. They taught her how to set and negotiate the fee comfortably – even though the fee was very low. They taught her when and how to best collect the fee. Laura was pretty good at this and none of her clients ever had a balance due on their account.

Since the agency where Laura worked before opening her practice was a government program, the average fee for a client seen there was only $8 per session. But Laura was really great at setting and collecting those $8 fees. When Laura left the agency, she still had the $8 fee figure in her mind. $8 had worked in the agency but $8 would not pay for her office rent. Laura asked other therapists what they thought she should charge. I don't recommend this as a business strategy and I'll explain why.

Laura's senior colleagues told her that, based on her limited years of experience, she should charge a much lower fee than her more experienced counterparts. Laura was also told that most people couldn't afford therapy so she should make sure her fee was low enough to help the poor people. She was also told that as a masters-level therapist, she should not charge too much since she didn't yet have a doctorate degree.

After some checking, she learned that many the senior therapists in her area were charging $125 - $175 per session in their private practices. Some were charging $100 per session and others, who were licensed many years, were charging as low as $75 a session. Entirely frustrated and confused, she came to me.

"What do *you* think you should charge?" I asked.

Laura thought for a bit and replied, "Well, I guess I shouldn't charge too much because there are people who have been doing this longer and they should get more than I do."

"Why? Do they do better work than you do?" I asked. She started to giggle and told me there were some excellent therapists in her area, but there were also some that had been licensed a long time and were just plain burned out.

I then asked her, "What else do you think the fee should be based on?"

"Well, every knows that PhDs should be paid more," she said.

"Why?" I asked. "Are the PhD's better at therapy than you are?"

Laura started to fidget. This conversation was becoming uncomfortable for her.

She continued. "Well, clients know that you're supposed to pay a PhD more than a master's level therapist."

"Really," I said. "You have been a master's level therapist in an agency for four years. How many clients have asked about your education level?"

"So what should I charge?"

I continued. "If there was no one else doing therapy in your town or even your state, what would you like to charge?"

She had an immediate response: "$150 a session."

Laura learned how to set that $150 fee with the same confidence that she did with her $8 fees. She decided to specialize in working with the wives of doctors. Since Laura had been the daughter of a physician, she knew the stress and unique concerns of families of physicians. She marketed to that target market and told me recently that more than 80% of her clients were paying her full fee. She said, "I believe in it and they do to."

How is your fee setting? If you'd like the specific scripts that my clients and I use to set, negotiate and collect fees, you may want to consider the "Be A Wealthy Therapist Implementation Kit." On page 323, you can see how to order and don't forget to use your discount coupon.

W I S D O M   N U G G E T

The fee that you set should be what you'd like to be paid to give up your free time and enter into the therapeutic relationship with this client.

After you check the state and federal legal and ethical standards for fee setting for your license type:

1. *Don't let others set your fee for you.*
2. *Don't assume that clients can't afford your fee.*
3. *Make sure you know your fee scale prior to discussing fees with a prospective client.*
4. *Never set a fee you will resent - no matter what else the client is doing with his or her money.*

Coaching Questions:

1. What do you believe your fee should be based on?

2. Where did you learn to set fees? How comfortable are you with your fee?

3. Have you spoken to your colleagues about their fee? If not, why not?

CHAPTER FOURTEEN

#5: Collect:
But She Couldn't Afford My fee

WISDOM NUGGET

Never, ever set a fee that will make you resent the client later
if you find they have money for other 'luxuries'.

If you're like most therapists, you have at least once offered a new
client a lower fee because he or she couldn't "afford" therapy.

And if you're like most therapists, there has been at least one
time that you found out that the client couldn't "afford" your full
fee, but did have money for vacations, cars or designer shoes.

And the resentment kicked in.

A colleague of mine, Pamela, was treating a lovely French-born
client named Monique. Monique was a single mom of two boys
and had a part-time job teaching French at the local community
college. Monique's husband had died of cancer at a very early age
six months prior and Monique had been unprepared to enter the
work force. She barely made enough to pay her rent and her sons'
tuition. In fact, Monique had recently sold her home and she and
her sons moved into a tiny apartment. This was so she could afford

to keep her sons in the private school they attended prior to their father's death.

Pamela's standard fee was $120 per session. But she was enchanted with Monique's accent over the phone and after hearing her story, Pamela offered Monique a fee of only $25 per session.

Therapy began, went well and Monique quickly became one of Pamela's favorite clients.

About three months into therapy, Monique told Pamela that she would be away for three weeks. She and her two sons were going to visit her family in France.

Monique did not know that Pamela had wanted to go to Paris ever since she first learned about the Eiffel tower in grade school. Pamela had taken art history courses in college to prepare for her "eventual" trip to France. She had a "dream journal" where she cut out pictures of the Eiffel tower and Parisian cafes. She read books on Paris and went on "virtual museum tours" on the Internet. She took French lessons from a neighbor.

Pamela was also a single mother and she had a lot of school loans she was repaying. There wasn't very much extra money. But she had been putting away $100 a month in her "Paris account" for over three years. Yet, she didn't have enough for Pamela and her daughter to make the trip.

But Monique - who was paying $25 a session - had enough money to go to France with her two sons.

In a nanosecond, Pamela went through a rollercoaster of emotions. She wanted to be happy for Monique - and she was. After all the pain Monique had been through over the last few months, some time with her family in familiar surroundings might be just what she needs. But Pamela couldn't help thinking, "That's my trip she's taking." There was a lump of resentment quickly followed by a feeling of guilt over the resentment.

Some therapists might have decided to increase Monique's fee. After all, she must have *some* money if she could afford a trip to

France. She must be able to pay a higher fee and she should "if she really valued therapy."

Not Pamela. She thought it through and decided that she - not Monique - had set the lower fee. (Monique may have suggested the amount, but it was Pamela who agreed.) Pamela decided she could not be angry with Monique for a decision that she - as the therapist/business owner - made.

Pamela went deeper. She realized that she was negatively judging Monique's priorities. She was assuming that, if Monique had extra money, it should go to therapy before a trip. In fact, Pamela concluded, her own thinking was actually a bit arrogant as a trip home to see family that she missed dearly might help Monique to heal in ways that therapy could not.

If a client tells you they have no money, it means they have no money they want to give you for therapy. And that's fine. Everyone gets to decide how to spend his or her own money. Your job is to never be resentful of the fees you set. It hurts you and it can interfere with you doing your best work with the client.

Pamela spent two weeks doing her "inner work" to become happy again for Monique and Monique's trip. She was able to celebrate with Monique when she left and heard all about her adventures when she returned. Monique, who still did not know of Pamela's desire to visit Paris, brought her a snow globe with the Eiffel Tower in it. Pamela told me that snow globe was her incentive to save more and she and her daughter did eventually make the trip. "It was a trip of a lifetime," they both tell me.

But that's not the end of the story. In one session after her trip, Monique confessed, "I am so lucky to have my family. They paid for our entire trip. I have no idea how I would have paid for it myself."

1. *I am not saying, don't offer lower fees. I hope sometimes you do. Just don't resent the fee you set if you find the client spending money elsewhere.*

2. *If you do set a fee you later resent, think of it as your gift in dirty paper. The gift is the reminder to only set fees you feel comfortable with regardless of how the client spends the rest of his or her money.*

Coaching Questions:

1. Have you set a fee that you resented? How did you handle it?

2. If your client spends money on something other than therapy, is it possible that expense might help them as much as therapy? (For example, *in vitro* fertilization, a vacation or an advanced degree?)

3. What did you think of Pamela's deeper work where she realized she ought not to be judging what she felt Monique should be doing with her money?

#6: Count:
The Money Game

A psychology professor's six-year-old son knocks at the door of his father's study. "Daddy", he says. "I need help with a math problem I couldn't do at school."

"Sure." the father says and smiles. "Just tell me what's bothering you."

"Well, it's a really hard problem: There are four ducks swimming in a pond, when two more ducks come and join them. How many ducks are now swimming in the pond?"

The professor stares at his son with disbelief: "You couldn't do that?! All you need to know is that 4 + 2 = 6!"

"Do you think, I'm stupid?! Of course, I know that 4 + 2 = 6. But what does this have to do with ducks!?"

Let's get your ducks in a row. How many clients do you really need? As therapists, we tend to put our purpose and the work ahead of our business planning. But if you want to be relaxed when your bills come, I recommend you set financial goals for your practice.

You can set your financial goals with some formulas. But let's make this fun – I call it "The Money Game." (There is a worksheet in Appendix B for you to play your own Money Game.)

(Math alert - there are some simple formulas here - if you have a little math anxiety, just take your time with them and follow Megan's example listed below.)

There are three variables to consider when looking at your income goals:

1. How much you wish to earn per year.
2. How many sessions you'd like to average per week.
3. What your average fee per session will be.

Let's look at the first variable:

1. How much you wish to earn per year.

While you may be tempted to pull a number out of the air for this, let's do it a little more scientifically. Add up all your expenses (monthly, irregular and annual ones) to determine how much you will need for a year. Be sure to include your business expenses including continuing education, insurance, and taxes. Include some for savings. If your business pays for your personal expenses – such as vacation, childcare or your mortgage - include these as well. Include any extra expenses or savings that you'd like cover with your private practice income. Now you have the amount you know you need to earn to pay your bills for a year. Let's call this your Annual Income Goal.

2. How many sessions you'd like to average per week.

Everyone has different ideas about the definition of a "full" practice. The choice is certainly up to you. Do you want a small practice seeing only five or ten clients per week or do you want a large practice seeing thirty or more clients per week? This is both an economic and a lifestyle choice.

3. What your average fee per session will be.

What are you charging now? When I ask this question of therapists, I usually am told their full fee. Then I ask, "Does everyone pay you that?" Most say "no."

There are lots of schools of thought on setting fees. Some clinicians offer one fee to all clients while others offer a sliding scale. Some therapists take third-party (insurance) reimbursement as payment for services. These are very personal decisions, but I want you to know what your current *average* fee is. Here is how to calculate your average session fee:

$$\text{(Total income for the week)}$$
$$\div \text{ (\# of sessions per week)}$$
$$= \text{Average session fee}$$

By the way, you may find this an eye-opening experience. Many practitioners find their average fee is less than they intuitively thought. Gary, a pastor and MFT in La Jolla, California told me that once he did this exercise, he became more skilled at setting his fees. He realized that continuing to offer lower fees to so many of his new clients reduced his average fee and thus he'd have to work a lot more hours to make the annual income he needed.

Determine Your Weekly Income Goal.

Now that you have your annual income goal, the number of sessions you wish to do per week and your average session fee, you're now ready for the income formulas.

Weekly Income Goal Formula: Calculate your target weekly income goal.

$$(\text{Annual Income Goal})$$
$$\div (44 \text{ Weeks})$$
$$= \text{Weekly Income Goal}$$

So you take the amount you wish to earn annually (your total business and personal expenses from #1 above) and divide by 44 weeks per year in order to determine how much you need to earn each week.

But wait, there are 52 weeks per year and I said divide by 44 weeks. Why 44? I recommend that people budget for and anticipate taking eight weeks off during the year. That leaves 44 weeks a year. You're going to take *eight* weeks off. How cool is that?

Unfortunately, I don't mean you will have eight weeks in Hawaii. What I mean is, you will probably take two weeks vacation, have some sick time and take some continuing education classes.

In other words, this will be time you're out of the office and unavailable to see clients.

I also want you to really be prepared for the times that the bottom will suddenly fall out of your practice. You know what I'm talking about. There are times when all of a sudden you look up and your entire caseload for that day or that week has cancelled out.

Do you work the week between Christmas and New Year's? Many therapists I know do, because they feel sorry for the people who are struggling during that time. It's not uncommon though, for half to three-quarters of the people who book during that time to cancel their appointments. This can be very scary if you plan on that money coming in.

Let's plan, not only for the expected expenses, but also for the unplanned lulls that are bound to occur. I suggest you do this by assuming you will have a full caseload only 44 weeks out of the year.

Back to our Weekly Income Goal Formula:

(Annual Income Goal)
÷ (44 Weeks)
= Weekly Income Goal

When you divide your annual income requirements by 44 weeks, you learn how much you need to earn each week. If you're like many therapists, you might find that's less than you're bringing in now. No worries. Let's look at how you can increase your weekly income.

There are several ways you will increase your income – add more clients, more sessions (or both), or increase session fees. (Of course you might also choose to offer products for sale and we will discuss that in an upcoming chapter.)

If this is confusing or if your math anxiety is creeping in, breathe slowly and deeply three times and let's look at an example. This is a fictitious example of a therapist's practice. Let's call her Megan.

Last week, Megan did six sessions. While she saw only five clients, she saw her client Mary S. twice, so she did a total of six sessions. Megan started her practice a while ago and it has been very part-time. She started her fee at $80 and has been slowly raising it (for new clients only of course) as her confidence builds. She now charges $125 to new clients, but still has some existing clients at lower fees.

Monday - Mary S. - $80
Tuesday - Frances N. - $80
Tuesday - Joe R. - $110
Wednesday - Mary S. - $80
Wednesday - Jessica M. - $125
Thursday - Betina J. - $125
Total income for the week = $600.
Total number of sessions for the week = 6.

To calculate her average session fee, Megan uses the Average Fee Per Session Formula:

(Total income for the week)

÷ (# of sessions per week)

= Average session fee

Megan's total income of $600 ÷ 6 sessions = $100 (Average fee per session)

This came as a little shock to Megan. She was thinking her fee was $125 so she expected she would earn $125 x 6 or $750 week. But when she did the math, she realized her average fee was only $100.

After tallying her expenses, and adding in money for irregular and unexpected expenses, Megan wants to earn an annual income of $50,000 this year. Let's look at Megan's income weekly income requirements using the Weekly Income Goal Formula:

(Annual Income Goal)

÷ (44 Weeks)

= Weekly Income Goal

Megan's $50,000 annual income goal ÷ 44 weeks per year = $1137 weekly income goal.

Thus Megan needs to earn $1137 per week to reach her annual income goal of $50,000.

Last week she earned $600. Megan starts to feel a little discouraged.

Intuitively then, we can see that Megan will need to increase her number of sessions per week (probably with new clients) or she will need to increase her average fee by making sure new clients pay a fee that's higher than her average fee. In other words, the variables that make up her income are:

(Number of weekly sessions)
x (average session fee)
= weekly income

Again, in order for Megan to increase her income, she needs to either increase her number of weekly sessions or increase her hourly rate.

1. She may either double her number of sessions (from 6 to 12 by getting some new clients) at her current average session rate:

12 sessions per week x $100 average fee per session = $1200 weekly income (which is more than the $1137 per week she needs) or

2. She can raise her average session rate by making sure any new clients come in at the $125 rate.

Let's look at a new week for Megan:

Monday - Mary S. - $80
Monday - new client A - $125
Tuesday - Frances N. - $80
Tuesday - Joe R. - $110
Tuesday - new client B - $125
Wednesday - Mary S. - $80
Wednesday - Jessica M. - $125
Wednesday - new client C. - $125
Thursday - Betina J. - $125
Thursday - new client D - $125

Total number of session for the week = 10.
Total income for the week = $1100.
Average session rate = $110.

By making sure the new clients paid the new rate, Megan needed only four new clients to get her closer to her weekly goal.

To calculate your income goals, use the Money Game Worksheet in Appendix B. Play with your numbers to see what you want and need. But try to have fun with it. After all, this is The Money Game.

Play your own Money game with the worksheet in Appendix B.

1. *Calculate what you wish to earn annually.*
2. *Calculate how much you need to earn weekly to attain that annual goal. (Assume 44 weeks a year of a full caseload.)*
3. *Calculate what you currently earn per week and your average session fee.*
4. *Increase your weekly income by increasing your number of sessions per week or your average session fee.*

Sounds good. But how do you get the clients?

That's what the rest of this book is all about. Once you know how much you need, you can build and implement your marketing plan. You are not shooting in the dark, hoping you will get a client. You have a roadmap.

WISDOM NUGGET

To stay motivated and focused, each week, track your number of sessions, your weekly income and your average session fee. You will always know how your practice is doing financially. You will begin to see where the seasonal lulls are in your practice, but you won't panic because now, you're saving for them.

Coaching Questions:

1. Do you find the math in this chapter a bit difficult? If so, who can you ask to help you figure out your actual and desired income goals?

2. When you compare your current weekly income to your desired income, how does it differ?

3. If you're discouraged by the numbers, not to worry. We all have to start somewhere. What can you do now to start seeing an increase in your weekly income?

#7: Enjoy:
The Prosperity Game

"I hope you never lose your sense of wonder..."
—LEE ANN WOMACK

WISDOM NUGGET

To motivate yourself to market your practice, it can be useful to consider how it *feels* to have more money - to imagine spending it in ways that bring you joy.

In the last chapter, we played The Money Game. This is where you look at your numbers to decide how much money you want to earn and how many hours you want to work to earn that money. I invite you to play it often – it will help you feel in charge of your income.

There is another game called "The Prosperity Game" that might be fun for you to play. I first read about it in the book, *Ask and it is Given* by Ester and Jerry Hicks. It is a light, playful, imaginary game and has helped many to move through blocks about money and get to a fun place of attracting more of it.

In The Prosperity Game, you are invited to create an imaginary bank account. We will call this your prosperity account. It isn't a real account that you have with a bank but you are going to make imaginary deposits into this account and write checks from it.

You can set up and keep track of the "money" in this account with a ledger book, in a spreadsheet, with an old check register or you can make it a "new, imaginary" account in your Quicken software. However – I want to be clear – no money will be changing hands – it will all be on paper (or in your computer.)

Each day, you will put a line item in your register indicating you have made a deposit. Then each day, you are to figure out how you would like to spend that money. Then you write an imaginary check (or place a line item in your register) indicating how you "spent" the money and calculate the new balance in your account.

It is best if you try and spend the money each day rather than saving it although there may be days you don't spend it all. The purpose of this game is to expand your imagination and to hopefully lessen some of the resistance to "having money."

Ready? On Day 1, "deposit" $100.

Then consider how you would like to spend this money. I said – spend. I encourage you not to regularly save the money in your prosperity account.

It is Day 1. You have $100 extra dollars – what would you like?

My group coaching clients shared some answers:

"I would like to buy some new art supplies and start painting again.'

"A massage."

"A fantastic dinner out with my mate complete with wine and dessert."

"My computer needs a new hard drive."

"I'd like to buy some very cool sneakers for my son."

Once you decide what you'd like to buy, I don't recommend you run out and actually buy it. Put a line item in your "Prosperity Account" register indicating that you "bought" this item (or service) and subtract the amount from your balance. You will either have a zero balance or perhaps, a very small amount left.

Now – stay with me here. Here is where it gets fun.

On Day 2, add $200 to your prosperity account bank register. Your balance should be roughly $200.

Now, how would you like to spend $200?

An iPod nano with some audio books loaded on to it?

A one-night stay in a hotel with your sweetie?

Kitchen toys?

Look up the exact cost of what you would buy. Write it in your check register for this account. You may decide you want to buy a couple of things. Enjoy looking and "spend it" from this prosperity account. Try to spend the whole balance each day.

Because guess what? You guessed it – on Day 3 you will put $300 into your account.

On Day 4, you will put $400 into your prosperity account.

On Day 5, you will put in $500.

If you do this for a month, you will have deposited $46,500 in your prosperity account. You will have the opportunity to enjoy "spending that money." If you continue to play it for a year, you will have deposited over six million dollars.

Let me check in with you here. How do you feel about playing The Prosperity Game?

Darlene told me, "When I started and put in the first deposit of $100, I felt fine. I could imagine spending it on my grandson with a day for the two of us at Disneyland. But after the third or fourth day, I hit a wall. I found myself saying 'I don't deserve this.' These were beliefs I didn't know I had and they were very eye opening.

I actually talked to my therapist about it and we worked through some issues of 'deserving.' I have played The Prosperity Game now for two months. The funniest thing has happened. Within a couple of weeks, I received some unexpected referrals – full fee ones. I love seeing the money come in now."

Again, this game is meant to be light and playful. Please enjoy it.

The purpose of The Prosperity Game is three-fold:

Revive your imagination. Remember when you were a child? How vivid our imaginations were then. Sometimes when we get older, we get so practical and lose our sense of wonder.

Work through any remaining issues of deserving.

Help yourself to allow more income to come to you.

Coaching Questions:

1. What comes up – emotionally – for you when you consider playing The Prosperity Game? Are you going to play it for at least one month?

2. If you find yourself feeling negative toward it, why do you think that is? Is it something you want to look at?

3. Would you like a way to play this online? I encourage you to visit: **http://www.choosingprosperity.com/game/**

SECTION FOUR

The Great Marketing Reframe

"If you don't like the way something looks,
change the way you look at it."
—WAYNE DYER

CHAPTER SEVENTEEN

Marketing = Community Service

"Marketing is icky - it feels like I am selling myself," my new coaching client Beth stated emphatically. "It feels way too narcissistic to put myself out there."

This is my favorite objection to marketing. It's also the easiest for me to answer.

If you have heard me speak on this before, you know where I am going with this. It's important to nip this concern in the bud because, if you don't, your phone simply will not ring.

WISDOM NUGGET

The people in your community deserve to know that you can help them. You must not keep yourself a secret.

Here is the good news:

You aren't marketing yourself.

You aren't even marketing your practice.

You're letting people in your community know you have the skills and desire to help people feel better in their lives and relationships.

Once, when I was out of town, I broke a tooth. I was so glad there was a local dentist that advertised "Emergency Dental Appointments." Within an hour, I was in and out and was able to enjoy the rest of my vacation.

When a pipe under my bathroom sink broke and flooded my house, I was glad that the "water cleanup and restoration" people marketed their business. They came quickly with huge vacuum cleaners and fans and dried out my carpets.

My husband Bob and I had no idea who to trust when it came to getting a new mortgage. Luckily I knew Becky from my networking group. I trusted her and the loan process with her was the easiest I had ever experienced.

It's absolutely essential that we reframe our view of marketing our practice. It isn't about being narcissistic or "ambulance chasing."

Marketing your practice is a service to your community.

When I am in a feisty mood and really want to drive this point home, I like to tell therapists, "If you're not marketing your practice, you're doing your community a *disservice*. You owe it to them to let them know there is hope and help."

Back to Beth, the new coaching client. Once she reframed marketing in this way - as a community service - she no longer felt marketing was as "icky and narcissistic." She got excited about letting those in her community see her joy and passion for the work. She separated the idea of talking about what she did from the "icky-ness of selling herself." She wasn't even "selling." She was "sharing." Talk about reframing!

You went to school for many years to learn therapeutic theories and interventions.

Depending on your license type, you probably spent between two and six years in internships for little or no pay. You most likely took a series of examinations designed to make sure the public has qualified practitioners to turn to when they are in pain. Now it's time to let the community know you're there to help them with their pain.

Coaching Questions:

1. If you have skills and the caring to alleviate a certain type of suffering, don't you owe it to those with that pain to let them know you're available to help them?

2. Have your thoughts about marketing changed any as a result of this chapter?

3. I encourage you to notice how your colleagues talk or respond to the idea of marketing. Are they positive or negative about it? Find one colleague with whom you can share your excitement about learning how to let the community see your passion for your work.

CHAPTER EIGHTEEN

Marketing = Giving

A new couple came into Brian's therapy office. They sat nervously on the couch. This couple had just received news that their daughter had been expelled from a prestigious private high school for using drugs on campus. He could see their concern, anger and hopelessness.

Brian relaxed in his chair and smiled.

"How can I help?"

They started to pour out their hearts. Brian listened empathetically and together the three of them came up with a game plan. Brian would meet with the daughter twice, then with the whole family once for an assessment. After the assessment, they would make a decision on what steps to take next.

It's second nature for therapists to enter a session - especially an intake session - with one simple concern: "How can I help?"

Let's move this same concern beyond the session within your office and out into the community.

It's almost irresistible when someone asks, "How can I serve you?"

Imagine going into a church and telling the staff who you are and asking, "How can I serve you?" I know several therapists who have done just that with great success.

I did that once with a church and they said something like, "You could teach the baptism ministry how to deal with difficult parents and, by the way, would you be willing to facilitate the annual staff team-building retreat?" Gosh, I didn't have to think about that one long – I imagined all the church staff that might lead to referrals. How is that for an opportunity? That led to facilitating a four-day retreat for the priests in my area.

In all my marketing, whether it's meeting with a potential referral source or writing my newsletter, I am always thinking, "How can I serve you?"

Paradoxically, when we take the focus off ourselves and show interest and concern in the other person, we end up with more clients. In a way, it seems counterintuitive - like turning a skidding vehicle *into* the skid in order to retain control.

Think about it. Your marketing efforts are intended to help people get to know, like and trust you. By asking how you can serve someone instead of asking for referrals, you will ultimately get referrals. Everyone loves a giver.

You might be thinking, "Casey, are you telling me to give away free therapy and volunteer all the time? What about making a good living?" I want to address that specifically. I am not suggesting you ever give away your time in a way that hurts you or your business.

This is about seeing what people need. Too often, those new to marketing go into a potential referral source armed with their credentials, resume and a 'talk' they'd like to give. What happens if someone already gave that talk last week? Before you can offer something of value to someone, you need to know what your potential referral source needs.

Months ago, a very nice man was building an Internet business marketing to therapists. He asked to interview me. His plan was to sell the CD of our interview. He thought he needed to offer me something in order for me to agree to do it. Here was his first proposal:

"You could send people who want to know more about your programs to my site. They would buy the CD from me and they would learn more about what you do you. You could get more coaching clients." The problem was I already sell my own CDs with the same information so that wasn't a real selling point. He tried again:

"Do you want to send people from your site to my site and give those people a discount on the CD of my interview with you?" Not really sure why I would do that. Another try:

"Do you want 10% of the profits from the CD sales?" "Hmmm. Let's see…" I thought. "Sell the same information on my own site for 100% of the profits or send my prospects to him and get 10% of the profits." It still wasn't doing it for me.

Despite all this I agreed to do it - he was a fabulous interviewer – he had great questions and he ran with it when we went off script, which made for a great recording. In the end, he asked for my feedback.

"The interview was great." I said. "You're a natural. My advice is: before you ask someone for something, find out how you can serve them."

I continued, "My mission is to spread the word that therapists can make a good, honest living helping people. I am looking for more ways to spread the word. I would like to speak to more graduate students. I would like more subscribers to my newsletter. That's what I am always looking for." Try to put yourself in the shoes of the other and ask, "How can I serve you?"

WISDOM NUGGET

Theodore Roosevelt said it best, "No one cares how much you know until they know how much you care." When you come from a, "How can I serve you?" place, people are attracted to you and want to know more about what you do.

Referrals come from relationships.

Try approaching each of your prospective clients with an attitude of, How can I help? This is your best marketing strategy. Approach your referral sources with this same attitude and stay in touch with them regularly.

As people see you wanting to be of service, you should find more referrals coming your way.

Coaching Questions:

1. Do you find yourself more relaxed about marketing your practice when you visualize yourself coming in with the attitude of 'serving', rather than trying to 'sell' yourself?

2. How can you implement this idea with a referral source, today?

3. Consider discussing this idea with a colleague. See how you both might use this approach to boost your incoming referrals.

CHAPTER NINETEEN

Marketing = Romance

My friend Carla was telling me about when she was single and trying to find a husband. We both used the "serial monogamy" technique to find a husband.

Are you familiar with this process? Here is how it goes:

Go on a first date with someone. Date only that person for two years. Break up. Repeat.

It took us both many, many years to get married using this strategy. Neither of us recommends it.

To get a marriage proposal, we need to date several people to find the ones we want to get to know more. First we narrow the list and find one we like. Then we build a relationship with him or her over time to see if that person is a good candidate for a long-term partner.

How does that relate to marketing?

We need to be in front of a lot of prospects in order for some of them to refer to us or hire us as their therapist.

We need to build *relationships* with others who serve our target market with non-competing services. *Relationships* - not one-time occurrences such as, "I went to the doctor's office and introduced myself and he still has not sent me anyone."

We need to go on a lot of first dates because, not everyone will be a good match for us. For example, we need to network, build strategic alliances or commit to speaking engagements with many different people in order for some of them to want to work with us.

Further, we need to keep in touch with those prospects on a regular basis via a newsletter or presentation in order to stay relevant in their mind. We need to have regular contact with our referral sources too, asking, "How can I serve you?"

Here Are Some Suggestions:

1. As you become known in your community, you will interact with potential clients and referral sources on a regular basis. In marketing, this is called "Filling your Pipeline." If you want water to flow into your house, you must have water in the pipe. If you want clients, you need to keep the pump primed, with prospects and referral sources in your pipeline. This means having a focused, structured marketing plan that you implement each week or month to make sure you're meeting these contacts.

2. Imagine that you saw a TV commercial or a print ad for a product only once. Would you remember that product? Of course not. You must keep in touch with your prospects and referral sources on a regular basis so that they remember you.

Marketing is so much like dating. You can go out on a 1,000 first dates and never have a second date with any of them.

Or you can "get married on the first date" and stay with someone not well suited to you for a very long time without letting others know whom you are and what you have to offer.

Neither of those are great options if you want to be happily married.

And it is exactly the same with building your practice.

W I S D O M N U G G E T

A lot of people need to know you in order for some of them to refer clients to you and in order for some of those referrals to become clients. While in some ways, it is about the quantity of people who know what you do; it is even more about the quality of the relationships you build with those people.

Get to know a lot of people in a structured, focused way.

Keep in touch with people who are interested in what you do in a way that is of value to them.

You can do this even if you are an introvert if you have a good plan and stay motivated.

Coaching Questions:

1. How many people do you think could articulate what you do?

2. Are they in a position to refer to you?

3. If you don't already have one, consider creating a 'stay-in-touch' plan with referral sources and prospective clients. For example, offer a free report or free audio to people who come to hear you speak. Get permission to email it to them after the event. That way you're beginning to build a relationship with them.

SECTION FIVE

The Four Marketing Personalities: What's Yours?

"The privilege of a lifetime
is being who you are."
—JOSEPH CAMPBELL

CHAPTER TWENTY

Good News! You Don't Have to be An Introvert

Alani, a colleague of mine, was raised in Hawaii and moved to the mainland when she was five. She's a very petite therapist and has a beautiful heart. She's also a very strong introvert. She never thought she'd be able to leave the agency where she worked and build a private practice. She, like many therapists, believed that marketing was all about giving out your business card to strangers at Chambers' of Commerce meetings and asking them for referrals. And it made her very uncomfortable.

But Alani really wanted a private practice. So she tried some alternative marketing strategies - ones that worked with her personality - and she built the practice she's always wanted. She did it and so can you.

I have found that many people think you have to be a full-blown extrovert to successfully develop relationships in the community. While being an extrovert is a distinct advantage, I have found that therapists tend to fall into four types of marketing personalities. No matter which one you most closely identify with, you can develop a marketing plan best suited for you. And believe me, when you do that, marketing is not so scary and is quite a lot easier than trying to be something you're not.

Here are the four types:

1. The Introverted Marketing Personality Type.

Alani is an introvert. She's great 'one-on-one' with folks. She loves deep conversations, but the thought of schmoozing with people she doesn't know is enough to drive her to hide under the table. But, Alani is fine at events that are structured. She started volunteering at a charity related to her specialty. By volunteering she was able to meet others who serviced her ideal client. (She met wealthy ones too.) Because she saw her volunteer work as giving back to the community, she was able to relax and enjoy herself. She didn't try to "sell herself." People would chat with her one-on-one and she would shine. She told them about her love for her work while sprinkling in some success stories and people started to refer to her. With her newfound confidence, Alani ventured out to some structured business networking groups. These are groups that have formal agendas, so Alani didn't have to think about standing around with a glass of Diet Coke wondering how to talk to all these people. The structured format helped her relax. Whenever she relaxed, people seemed to want to talk to her. Her practice continues to grow today using these strategies.

2. The Techno Lover Marketing Personality Type.

Techno Lovers are clinicians who feel as comfortable as a junior high school student at the keyboard. Techno Lovers understand that many, many people will be searching the web looking for counselors. They fuss with their website adding very effective bells and whistles. They write tips to their niche market on a Blog. They're listed on several online therapist locator sites such as **www.Find-A-Therapist.com** and **www.Counsel-Search.com.** If you're a Techno Lover, you're really lucky and way ahead of the game. Overwhelmed by technology? Not to worry. There are a lot of people you can cajole (your teenage daughter, for example) or hire, to get you set up with an online presence.

3. The Creative Marketing Personality Type.

Remember in high school when you were trying to figure out how to decorate the gym for the prom? A few students on the prom committee turned the boring gym into "New York Night Life" with tinsel stars on the ceiling, champagne glass with fake bubbles on the tables and a very cool papier-mâché Statue of Liberty? Some of those students became therapists. I call them the Creative Marketing Personality Types. They love to create things of beauty. They make beautiful "nice to meet you" or "thank you for the referral" notes. When they send these notes to potential and existing referral sources, they stand out and are remembered. When a Creative Marketing Type gives a community presentation, the attendees get a hands-on experience and often leave with an inexpensive promotional favor that reminds them of the experience (and the therapist.)

4. The Extroverted Marketing Personality Type.

Alani (and me too, for that matter) envy the Extroverts. They are at ease in a roomful of strangers and can start conversations with just about anyone. Both casual and business networking are second nature to the Extroverted Marketing Type. They can talk to almost anyone about their passion for their work. The bottom line is that marketing a practice is easier in many ways for Extroverted Marketing Types than the rest of us. We all have our gifts and Extroverts do have an advantage here.

I hope this discussion of the Marketing Personality Types makes you feel more hopeful about marketing your practice. You don't have to be a strong extrovert to be successful in getting fee-for-service clients. You can be true to yourself and your personality, while building the practice you really want. That's exactly what Alani did.

WISDOM NUGGET

No matter which of the four Marketing Personality Types you most identify with, you can have great success (and even a good time) marketing your practice. Just learn the strategies and experiment with what works for you, your niche market, and your community.

There are four different Marketing Personality Types:

1. *The Introverted Marketing Personality Type*
2. *The Techno Lover Marketing Personality Type*
3. *The Creative Marketing Personality Type*
4. *The Extroverted Marketing Personality Type*

All four Personality Types have their inherent advantages. Most of us have qualities of more than one type. Just use the strategies that work best for your personality type. Have a plan and play to your strengths.

Coaching Questions:

1. Prior to reading this chapter, did you worry that marketing your practice might be really hard because you thought your personality was not suited for it?

2. While most of us have some qualities of two or three of these personality types, which Marketing Personality Types best describes you?

3. Now that you know you don't have to be a strong extrovert, how can you change your marketing strategy?

CHAPTER TWENTY-ONE

#1
Champion Your Introverted Nature!

If you're an Introverted Marketing Personality Type, you probably already know it. Just in case you're uncertain, here are some traits of the Introverted Marketing Type:

1. When you think of marketing your practice, you sometimes consider running for the hills. You might be worried that marketing means you have to make 'small talk' which feels uncomfortable and a waste of time.

2. If your friend invites you to a networking meeting, you might either "have another engagement" or ask your friend about how the group is run and structured. If you know what to expect and it doesn't feel too threatening, you may consider it even though you'd rather not go.

3. You'd prefer to receive most of your client referrals from former clients or colleagues, friends and acquaintances. After all, they know you and know how well you do this work.

4. When encouraged by your coach to connect with a potential new referral source you think, "I'll write a note inviting them to call me if they want to get together. I don't want to call them; they may see it as a bother."

5. A really simple website with a place where potential clients can call you or email you if they want an appointment seems like a very good online presence.

6. If you had to market your practice, you'd probably prefer to ask a trusted colleague for referrals rather than speak to a large group of people.

7. When a friend suggests putting your practice information on an online therapist locator (such as **www.Find-A-Therapist.com**), you ask your close confidants how it's working for them. Then, you might view the discussion forums to see how the service is working for others.

8. If invited to do a large speaking event, you'd most likely say, "no", freak out, or write out your talk in detail ahead of time, so you'll feel more confident.

9. The idea of visiting doctors' offices, churches or schools is not appealing at all.

10. You're at your best when you can have deep conversations, at one-on-one meetings, with people you really care about.

WISDOM NUGGET

Even though it may appear at first that marketing is the most difficult for Introverted Marketing Personality Types, it's the Introvert's desire to get the spotlight off themselves that can actually be the very best and most effective marketing technique. Introverts can actually be some of the best private practice marketers.

How To Market Your Practice As An Introvert:

1. Review Section 7 where we match the marketing activities with the Marketing Personality Types. Select two that are recommended for Introverts and give them a try.

2. Recognize that being an Introvert gives you a distinct advantage in your marketing efforts - people easily talk about themselves around you.

3. Develop a list of questions that you can ask potential referral sources and prospects. With these questions in your mind, it'll be easier to talk to people.

4. If marketing makes your stomach knot up, this one little secret can turn you into a business magnet - with little or no effort. Never try to sell yourself. Always come from your very natural, *"How can I serve you?"* place.

As an Introverted Marketing Personality Type, it may take a little longer for you to become known in your community, but you can still build a fantastic practice.

Most people love to talk about themselves.

This gives Introverts a distinct advantage. Introverts can easily invite people to talk about themselves in a way that makes potential referral sources want to refer to them.

Celebrate your Introverted personality.

Coaching Questions:

1. How can you reframe your ability to get people talking about themselves as a very special marketing trait you have?

2. Describe a time when people sought you out to confide in. Why do you think they did that?

3. Who can help you stay on track with your marketing? It's easiest for the Introverted Marketing Type to get off track and we want you to stay motivated.

CHAPTER TWENTY-TWO

#2

Techno Lovers Do it Bit By Bit

I was watching the grade school kids get on the school bus the other day. They were either listening to their iPods, or texting on their cell phones. Yesterday, at The Apple Store™, I saw four-year olds happily playing at the "kid's table" full of Mac computers. Clearly, technology is our future. If this idea excites you, you're a true Techno Lover. Here are some traits of the Techno Lover Marketing Personality Type:

1. When you want to improve your marketing efforts and results, you add new copy and features to your website.

2. When your friend invites you to a networking meeting, your first look up the group on the web to see what you can learn about them.

3. You'd like to receive most of your client referrals online. It's easy, effective and it's where you shine.

4. After meeting a potential referral source, you'd most likely follow up with an email rather than a phone call or note.

5. Your ideal online presence consists of an interactive website with very cool features such as an audio welcome message, an appointment scheduler and a place for them to sign up for

your online newsletter. It would be great to create an online community where web visitors could ask you questions.

6. Learning about pay-per-click website advertising appeals to you more than attending a networking meeting or giving a community presentation.

7. When a friend suggests putting your practice information on an online therapist locator (such as **www.Find-A-Therapist.com**), you immediately see the value and check into it.

8. If invited to present at a speaking event, you'd be more likely to ask if they have a Power Point projector than how early you can arrive to network.

9. You most likely have a Blog and your practice is listed on at least a couple of online therapist locator sites.

10. You're at your best when you can solve problems - and you really enjoy doing that at the computer.

WISDOM NUGGET

Technology will be, as I have said, the number one way we attract clients in the coming decade. People will be Googling for a therapist rather than using the Yellow Pages.

How To Market Your Practice As A Techno Lover:

1. Review Section 7 where we match the marketing activities with the Marketing Personality Types. Review the list for Techno Lover Personality Types and find two you're not currently doing and would like to try.

2. Make sure your website is 80% about the client and only 20% about you and your services. Remember - the client cares most about "Do you get me?" Speak to the client. Let them know you understand their pain and want to help them.

3. Put audio and/or a short video on your website. Let your prospects get a sense of who you are and what you look and sound like. This gives them the opportunity to decide if they want more from you.

4. Do you have something free that you will give away to your web visitors?

Warning – Danger Will Robinson: If you're a Techno Lover Personality Type, make sure you're working on marketing activities that will help you attract clients. It's very easy to spend a lot of time making minor changes to your website that will not help you get clients. Know what I mean?

Technology is wonderful and if you enjoy it, then you're very lucky.

Even if you don't love technology, have some type of online presence be a part of your marketing plan.

You will be way ahead of the curve.

Coaching Questions:

1. Consider doing other types of therapy - such as online therapy. Does the idea excite you or make you nervous? Why?

2. Some find their interest in technology both a strength and a weakness. Is that true for you? If so, how?

3. If you're not in love with technology, but still see the value in marketing your practice online, whom could you enlist for help?

CHAPTER TWENTY-THREE

#3
The Beauty of Creatives

"Creativity is inventing, experimenting, growing, taking risks, breaking rules, making mistakes, and having fun."
—Mary Lou Cook
(American community activist, calligrapher and author)

Are you a Creative Marketing Personality Type? Do you naturally enjoy creating beautiful things? Do your friends ask you for advice on how to design their business cards? Here are some traits of the Creative Marketing Personality Type:

1. When you think of marketing your practice, you imagine creating a beautiful practice brochure or other marketing piece.

2. When you're invited to attend a networking meeting, you'd like to design a lovely flyer to take with you.

3. You'd like to receive most of your client referrals from people you've met who share your energy.

4. When meeting a potential referral source, you'd enjoy following up with them by sending then a handmade card.

5. Your ideal online presence would be a gorgeous website whose design reflects your vision, energy and passion.

6. Having a free workshop with a lot of fun and experiential exercises appeals to you as a good marketing activity.

7. When a friend suggests listing your practice information with an online therapist locator (such as **www.Find-A-Therapist.com**), you ask if you can add your own style or design to your listing.

8. If invited to do a speaking event, you'd be most likely to design a handout or exercise that reflects your passion and energy.

9. You have a lot of hobbies outside the office that you enjoy.

10. You're at your best when you create something of beauty and joy.

WISDOM NUGGET

Creative Marketing Personality Types can be either introverted or extroverted folks. What motivates them most is their hunger to express their passion creatively.

How To Market Your Practice As A Creative:

1. Review Section 7 where we match the marketing activities with the Marketing Personality Types. Review the list for Creative Marketing Personality Types and find two that you strike you as fun.

2. Appreciate your gifts and vow to use them in your marketing.

3. While you want to capitalize on your creative gifts, make sure you keep track of where your referrals are coming from so you know where to continue to focus your marketing efforts.

4. Develop a method of keeping in touch with your prospects and referral sources that showcase your personality - hand-designed "nice to meet you" cards, hand-made gifts for referral sources, an electronic newsletter for your clients and prospects designed with your personality in mind.

Creatives bring a special joy to the world and can be natural marketers. Don't forget to keep in touch with your prospects and referral sources once a month.

The Creative Marketing Personality Type has an advantage over some of the other personality types.

People will remember the beautiful pieces or experiences that you create.

Make sure your contact information is on everything you create.

1. How might your gifts both help you succeed and potentially get in your way?

2. What products can you create to supplement your work and your income?

3. Do you make it a habit to let people see the joy you have for your clients and your work. If not, why do you think that is?

CHAPTER TWENTY-FOUR

#4
Extroverts Network Naturally

My stepmother Barbara is the most extroverted person I know. She loves meeting new people and everyone loves her. Once, when she and my dad went to Oregon on vacation, Barbara read in the paper that a local church was having a potluck and inviting the community. Barbara made a dish and went to the event. She had a ball. Truth be told, when I walk into a room of strangers, I will sometimes pretend I am Barbara. I act like she would - approaching people and introducing myself with a smile and asking where they're from. My initial nervousness disappears rather quickly.

If you're an Extroverted Marketing Personality Type, then you're quite blessed. Most of the rest of us are very envious of your ease with people. Here are some traits of the Extroverted Marketing Personality Type:

1. When you think of marketing your practice, you enjoy calling your colleagues to brainstorm.

2. You enthusiastically say, "Yes" when your friend invites you to a networking meeting.

3. You'd like to receive most of your client referrals from colleagues, friends and acquaintances. It's especially fun when you can "case share" with someone you really like.

4. When meeting a potential referral source you're likely to think, "I'll call and invite them to coffee or lunch."

5. Some days you wonder if you really need a website.

6. Speaking to a room full of your ideal clients is a marketing activity that might appeal to you.

7. When a friend suggests putting your practice information on an online therapist locator (such as **www.Find-A-Therapist.com**), you call your colleagues and ask them if it's really worthwhile.

8. If invited to do a speaking event, you'd probably show up early to network.

9. When you really think about it, you know a significant number of people.

10. You're at your best when you have the opportunity to socialize with a lot of wonderful people.

WISDOM NUGGET

Extroverts can be the life of any party and quite engaging. Use your strengths to get people to open up and talk about themselves. Invite others to be in the spotlight with you.

How To Market Your Practice As An Extrovert:

1. Review Section 7 where we match the marketing activities with the Marketing Personality Types. Review the list for Extroverted Marketing Personality Types and find two activities to implement.

2. When chatting with others, invite them to talk about themselves first. You can use your ease with people to invite less extroverted people to talk about themselves, thereby endearing people to you.

3. Develop a signature talk that speaks to your ideal client. Make sure you have something to offer attendees so they can get more information from you.

4. Create your 'keep in touch' strategy and calendar it. Make sure you stay in touch with prospects and potential referral sources at least once a month.

My dad tells me that wherever they travel - no matter what country they are in - it's highly likely that they will meet someone Barbara knows. How is this possible? Not only is she interested in others, she keeps in touch with those she meets. She's interested in their lives. Maybe you've met her - Barbara Perriman.

The Extroverted Marketing Personality Types have a distinct advantage over some of the other Marketing Personality Types. Their natural ease in new situations and their desire to connect with others makes marketing a practice pretty simple. By learning a few simple techniques, Extroverts can use their natural marketing gifts and build a fantastic practice.

Coaching Questions:

1. How can being an Extroverted Marketing Personality Type be both a strength and a weakness?

2. As an Extrovert, what are you doing now to market your practice? What else might you consider?

3. Do you have a system (formal or informal) for keeping in touch with people you've met? If not, how might it be helpful to your practice-building efforts?

SECTION SIX

Choose Your Clients

"It's choice - not chance - that determines your destiny"
—JEAN NIDETCH

CHAPTER TWENTY-FIVE

What Do They Want From You?

Amy said to me, "I know you want me to specialize, but I don't want to. My ideal population is…." She thought for a second and said, "…humans."

I laughed so hard the tears came, but I understood her reluctance. Therapists don't want to exclude anyone. They worry that if they market a specialty, they will be denying help to someone. However, nothing is further from the truth. You want to pick a specialty for marketing purposes, but you will see lots of different types of clients and problems in your practice - whether you specialize or not.

Amy told me she had taken some training in sex therapy and was considering marketing a sex therapy practice. Then she said, "But I really enjoy working with adolescent girls too, so I think I will market both specialties."

I was imagining her business card: "Counseling for adolescent girls. Sex therapy." Now that could cause some confusion.

In earlier chapters, I wrote that people are coming to therapy these days to have problems solved - but it's the problem from the *client's* point of view.

Many therapists make the mistake of thinking that marketing a specialty means marketing a DSM diagnosis. The general public (on the intake call) doesn't request therapy because of a DSM diagnosis. In my entire history of practicing, only two clients on the intake call indicated they wanted help with a specific DSM diagnosis. (Although I will admit that, with the advent of TV commercials for psychopharmacological drugs, this has increased.)

What do they want from you? What problems do they need help with? Look at your intake notes. Why do people say they came for help? Look at your ideal clients - what did they say on the intake? Not now, after they have been in treatment, but on the intake call.

WISDOM NUGGET

While there are certainly people seeking therapy because they are searching for existential meaning in their lives, the therapists I coach have found that most people come into therapy for one of two reasons:

1. To have someone else change, and/or
2. To have something else change.

Here are some examples. I am sure you have encountered these a time or two:

"My spouse doesn't communicate with me."

"I am worried about my teen. He seems to be making bad choices."

"My boss is on my back and I think I am going to lose it one of these days."

"My husband just told me he's gay."

Again, there are certainly exceptions to this, but I imagine if you look over your notes, you'll find a preponderance of these types of complaints.

What does this mean for you? To build your practice faster and keep it full, I recommend you market to a specialty.

Why? Because you want to be "memorable." You want to stand out from the other therapists. Look at it from your client's point of view. Why should a client pick you over the 700 other therapists in your community? What makes you more desirable?

What do your clients want? It's not your credentials. It's not your years of experience. They want to know if you *get them*. They want to know you understand their problem - not the diagnosis - but the problem as *they* see it.

The best way to pick which specialty to market is by choosing: a type of person, a problem, or a person with a problem. Here are some examples:

Types of people:

- CPAs
- Women executives
- First time moms
- Dads

Problems:

- Fear of flying
- An affair
- Loss of a loved one
- People who have "issues with food"
- Sharing custody

Person with a problem:

- Couples who are tired of arguing
- Couples who want to be part of the 50% of people who stay together
- Women who desperately want a baby

- Dads who share custody of their kids
- Christians who have lost someone they love

You get the idea. The specialty is not a DSM diagnosis - it's a problem from the client's point of view.

A special note here: A lot of people have advanced training in various processes such as EMDR, Art Therapy, Somatic Experience, etc. I don't recommend you try selling a *process*. Most people want a solution to a problem - not a process.

People will wake up at 3 a.m. worrying about *their problem* - not *your solution*. I often tell stories of my dental experiences. One time during a root canal, the dentist was training a new assistant. She gave the new assistant a play-by-play of what she was doing in my mouth. I did not want to know the details of *how* she was going to make me feel better - I just wanted her to do it. I freaked out when she said, "Okay, now we'll burn the tissue with the laser - everyone look away." (By the way, my new dentist has an iPod for me to listen to during my visits. Much better.)

Don't try to sell a process. People don't always want to know *how* you're going to help - just *that* you're going to help. Marketing a process just adds the extra step of explaining why the process fixes the problem. Start with the problem and then bring up your process solution if you feel it's necessary.

I think Amy will settle on specializing in sex therapy although, she's not using those words when people ask her what she does, as they can easily end a conversation.

She's coming up with a plan to connect with urologists, OB-GYNs and internists. I know she's going to succeed.

To attract more clients (especially fee-for-service clients) you need to market a specialty - a specialty from the client's point of view.

What problem wakes your client up at 3 a.m. and makes them want to pay you to help them solve it? When you answer that, you have your specialty and half of your marketing vocabulary complete.

Coaching Questions:

1. Does the idea of marketing a specialty make you uncomfortable?

2. What would you need to believe in order for it to feel better?

3. Consider interviewing two therapists who are known for a specialty. Tell them your concerns and see if they have some answers for you.

CHAPTER TWENTY-SIX

How It's Done 101:
Proof it Works

In the last chapter we talked about specializing. Many therapists feel it's difficult to build a practice if they market to just one specialty. I'd like to share with you a story about my colleagues Dr. Ellyn Bader and Dr. Pete Pearson.

If you haven't met Ellyn and Pete, make it a point to do so. They are the founders and directors of The Couple's Institute in Menlo Park, California. They are the creators of the Developmental Model Of Couples Therapy and you have probably read their quintessential texts on the subject *In Quest of the Mythical Mate* and *Tell Me No Lies*. They are world-renowned experts on helping couples have really great relationships and, in helping therapists build thriving practices working with couples.

In 1983, Ellyn and Pete decided they wanted to have a business together, but they weren't sure what it would be. They threw around a bunch of ideas including opening a restaurant. Ellyn says it took a while, but they decided they did have a big passion for couple's therapy but they worried if they could make a go of it with just one specialty. In fact, Ellyn told me, "The idea of focusing on just working with couples seemed challenging and threatening. Everyone told us we couldn't make a living being that specialized." Pete told me, "Back then, we were told that if we specialized in couples, we would have to work nights and weekends because couples couldn't come for therapy during the day. We found that simply was not true."

Specializing is exactly what has helped Ellyn and Pete build a thriving practice and they now have many therapists working for them. Over the years they have developed a variety of services, products and resources for professionals and the public. They write books, present training workshops, sell professional CD programs and more - all focused on couples. I love to pick their brains about their success because we can all take a page out of their book. They have figured out, a lot of it by trial and error, what works and they continue doing so. They were willing to take a gamble and specialize when many of the rest of us were scared to do so.

The Couples Institute continues to grow and fulfill their mission by marketing counseling services to the general public. A lot of their marketing these days is via the Internet. While they have two websites, one for couples and one for clinicians, let's look at the website for couples seeking help: **www.TheCouplesInstitute.com**

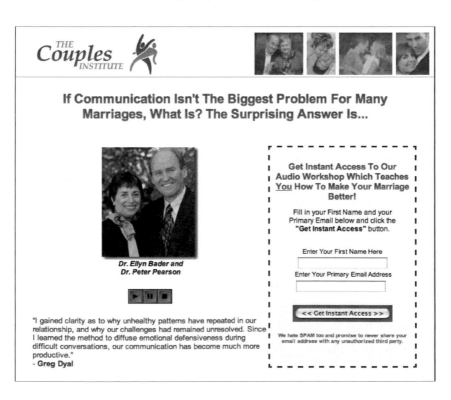

The home page of this site is lovely and very simple. There is a short entertaining audio that invites the web visitor to get a longer recording at no charge. In the audio, Pete keeps telling me that if I am having communications problems in my relationship, it's not my fault. (I had to have my husband Bob listen to that one.)

When the web visitor fills in his name and email address, in order to get another free recording, he will also get a newsletter regularly with tips on improving relationships. This "keep in touch" strategy helps people keep The Couples Institute in mind when they are ready for counseling. These tips are sent in an audio format. By hearing Ellyn and Pete's voices, the web visitors get a sense of their style. A sense of familiarity begins to develop - even before they call for an appointment.

The Couples Institute is a perfect example of a therapy practice that has built a strong reputation by specializing. They were told they couldn't do it, but they have, and they continue to grow everyday.

Ellyn and Pete also feel a strong need to give back to the profession. Many therapists are treating couples (often very difficult couples) without the benefit of specific training. Couples therapy is often very demanding as they are coming in as a last resort when they are feeling at their most angry and bitter. If you want to really be effective with couples, it's important to know how to treat the couple exactly where they are at the moment and to care for yourself in the process.

Ellyn and Pete have created several training programs for couple's therapists. They offer in-person workshops, group Tele-class trainings and home study courses. My favorite is *In Quest of the Mythical Mate* - a comprehensive practice building kit in a box for therapists who want to build a successful practice with couples. Starting with 10 audio CDs and a 96-page workbook, this program teaches diagnosis, first sessions, managing tough couples and other specific techniques. It has lots of actual transcripts and clinical vignettes, and real examples of sessions sprinkled throughout the CDs to demonstrate what you're learning. It serves as a foundation for therapists of all theoretical orientations. Check it out at **http://www.couplesinstitute.com/professional/products.html.** You can also sign up there for your free subscription to the *Practice Development Dispatch*. Every month you'll receive tips from Ellyn and Peter on the best ways to counsel and build your practice.

WISDOM NUGGET

Find out what you love and what people will pay for. Be focused. Be courageous. Don't listen to people who say you can't do it or they will be right. Create a marketing plan and track your results. Do what works.

A dynamite marketing plan - including speaking, networking and the Internet has helped The Couples Institute become a thriving business for over 25 years. As Ellyn and Pete began to run out of therapy hours, they added other therapists to their practice and created other products. This increased their income and allowed them to make an even bigger community contribution.

Coaching Questions:

1. When you read the story of The Couples Institute, what does it bring up for you?

2. Have you worried that specializing might limit your practice? Can you imagine that your practice might actually build faster if you pick and become known for a specialty?

3. Has a specialty found you rather than the other way around? If so, how do you feel about it?

CHAPTER TWENTY-SEVEN

More Proof:
Your Turn to Try It Yourself

Three other coaches and I recently had the honor of being on a panel of "blue chip coaches." We were there because all four of us had clearly identified niche markets. We talked about how we had tried to be more general in the beginning and found the more narrow our specialty, the more successful we became. We talked about how it was important to know what our clients (in that niche) want.

WISDOM NUGGET

To have a financially successful practice, you must offer something people want (and want to pay for).

The panel was a lot of fun and there was a great discussion about specializing. David is a "Hollywood Coach." His clients wanted their coach to know about the trials and tribulations of the industry. He said he was finding that even "Hollywood" was turning out to be too broad a niche specialty. Now, he's marketing 'sub-specialties' such as, "Television Head Writers."

Terri is a "Family Aging Dynamics Coach." She works with those who are care-giving their aging relatives. She helps them with the emotional and practical side. Terri shared an epiphany with us. When she first started her coaching business and talked about what she did, people associated her with "dying." She discovered that people didn't want to talk to her because it brought up uncomfortable feelings about aging and death. It was tough for Terri to get clients. She decided instead, to focus on *living more*. Once Terri reframed it, people became interested and she now has a thriving practice.

It's great to follow your interest and pick a specialty niche to market, but in order to make money you need to make sure it's something people will pay you for.

Many therapists have told me they work with "women in transition." While it sounds interesting, I am not sure what a "transition" is. I am sure I have been through a zillion transitions in my life, but I don't think I ever woke up at 3 a.m. thinking, "Gosh, I should get a therapist to help me with this transition." When I woke up at 3 a.m. worrying, it was because I was upset and wanted someone (or a situation) to change.

So how do we know what people will pay for? This is where the ideal client profile comes into play. I invite you to create a full vignette about a fictitious ideal client. Make it a story about a person (or a couple, or a family.) Give them a name, age, hair color, eye color, occupation, etc. Do they have pets? Children? If so, what are their names? What hobbies do they have? What is their level of community involvement? Most importantly, what do they wake up worrying about at 3:00 a.m.? You may be wondering why I don't suggest you base your ideal client on a real person. There seems to be too many opportunities for transference issues that can occur by doing so. Create a fictitious one - one you really, really like.

Then take your fictitious, ideal client to Starbucks for a Gestalt conversation. Ask her, "If you heard I work with (fill in your specialty here), would you want to see me and pay my full fee?" Your fictitious ideal client will tell you "yes", "no", or "maybe." Keep refining your specialty niche until you hear, "Yes!"

Again, it may sound like we'll be excluding others in our practice if we develop this ideal client profile. Nothing could be further from the truth. When people see you with a specialty, they respect you more and you'll attract more clients - ones with different problems, as well as the specialty you're marketing.

Once you know who your ideal client is and what they worry about, you will begin to know the best ways to market to them.

Make sure what you're offering, is what people want to buy.

After you have a specialty niche to market, develop an ideal client profile.

Then find out if your fictitious ideal client would want to pay for what you are offering.

Coaching Questions:

1. Create an ideal client profile as described above. Try to make the profile one person rather than a group of people such as, "women aged 30 - 60."

2. If you find you have a couple of different ideal clients, create two profiles and then see what they have in common.

3. If you find yourself uncomfortable with this exercise, is it because you're trying to serve everyone? Remember, the intention is not to exclude anyone. It's to develop a specialty niche that people will want to pay you to help them with.

CHAPTER TWENTY-EIGHT

A Word About Filling Your Practice Through Insurance Companies

I received a surprise call one day. It had been many years since I had spoken to this particular client. He said: "I need to come back and see you for a few sessions."

He agreed to the fee (at the time it was $150 per session) and we set an appointment. We met for two sessions. On the third session, he came in very excited.

"I just called my insurance company and it seems you're a provider on my panel. The lady was very nice - she backdated the authorization to my first session. Isn't that great?" he said.

Whoa. I had not seen any insurance clients for so long, I didn't even know I was still on any insurance company panels.

Very long story short - I had to refund to him the $300 he had already paid for the first two sessions since the insurance company was now going to pay for those sessions. The insurance rate was $60 per session. I saw him for a total of five sessions. I billed the insurance company exactly $300 for the five sessions. It took me six months (and several phone calls over the months) to get paid.

This is the main problem if you try to have a "hybrid practice." A "hybrid practice", is a practice where some clients are insurance company clients and some come from the therapist's own marketing efforts.

WISDOM NUGGET

If you have a hybrid practice, problems can arise. If you do the marketing to get the client and they wish to use insurance to pay for therapy, you're bound under your contract to accept the insurance rate for your fee. Ultimately, you're competing with yourself.

To get on panels or not? It's a great debate. Let's face it - someone has to market your practice. Either you can get out there and do it yourself or you can try and get on insurance panels. If you wish to use the insurance companies, then you sign a contract agreeing to their terms. They, in turn, put your contact information on their provider list and you may get some clients from it.

Some people think that this will fill their practice. If you have been on insurance panels for a long time, you may find that your practice is full with managed care clients. However, if you're starting out, know that it can take up to nine months to get your application approved. Know also, that you will be competing with others who have been on the panels longer than you have.

That said I have to share a pet peeve of mine. It really bothers me when clinicians complain about the low fees and extra paperwork that comes with being on managed care panels. It is not managed care that's causing the problem. If you have signed up to be on a panel, you agreed to their terms. You (overtly or covertly) decided that it was in your interest to have the insurance companies list your practice on their site. That was marketing you did not have to do. So be happy someone is doing that marketing or decide if you're benefiting enough to stay on the panels.

Some people feel they will work less if they get off the managed care panels since one fee-for-service client may pay you as much as two insurance clients together. Actually, it seems to work out about the same.

You get to make a choice - do you want to spend your time marketing or do you want to spend your time seeing managed care clients? You make the call.

The managed care panels work for you. They are, in a way, your outsides sale force. You agreed to a lower fee and more paperwork and they agreed to list your practice. If you do not like the job they are doing for you, fire them by resigning from the panel. Otherwise, be happy they are bringing you clients. They are fulfilling the contract that you agreed to.

Coaching Questions:

1. How do you feel about marketing your practice vs. having the managed care panel's list your practice?

2. How can you (or any therapists you know) avoid getting caught up in the "blame game" with managed care?

3. In your vision, do you have a managed care practice, a fee-for-service practice or a hybrid practice? Why?

SECTION SEVEN

Your Marketing Buffet

"It will never rain roses: when we want to have
more roses we must plant more trees."
—George Eliot

CHAPTER TWENTY-NINE

Your Marketing Plan Checklist

As a strong "J" on the Myers-Briggs Personality Inventory, I need to have lists - all kinds of lists. But my favorites are checklists. It helps me to be more focused. And I get very excited when I get to check something off.

If you're just getting starting marketing your practice (or you're wanting to do a more focused job of it) here are the steps my coaching clients and I use. Check them off as you go. I strongly suggest you do the steps in the order listed below. This will save you significant time and frustration later.

❑ 1. Create the vision of your practice. How many hours do you want to work? Which hours? Do you take managed care? Write out what you want your practice to look like.

❑ 2. Determine your ideal client. Remember, you're picking an ideal client for marketing purposes only. Of course you can see anyone you wish in your practice (and you will attract different types of clients), but I encourage you to pick one type of client to market to. It makes the most of your marketing time and dollar. Once you know to whom you're marketing, it's easier to talk about what you do in a way that prospects and referral sources "get".

❑ 3. Translate what you do into words that the ideal client

would resonate with and want to pay for. It's easy to use clinical terms when describing who you help. Don't label yourself as a social worker or a psychologist. You're a person who relieves a particular kind of pain. Speak from your ideal client's point of view and reference their pain. For example, "I am a special kind of counselor. I help frustrated parents and teens get along." Or, "I teach husbands how to 'get' their wives." Or, "I work with people who are afraid of going to the dentist." You want to use the words that the client would use - again, words that the ideal client would resonate with and want to pay for.

❏ 4. Determine where your client hangs out and who else services them. Once you have picked a specialty for marketing purposes, you can begin to draft your marketing plan. You will want to be in the community in places where your ideal client is and begin to develop referral relationships with them and with others who serve them.

❏ 5. Review possible marketing activities - including those listed in this book and others that you want to try.

❏ 6. Select the marketing activities that work best for your personality, your market, and your community - including at least one 'keep in touch' activity. Many possible marketing activities are listed in the next chapter.

❏ 7. Determine the tasks that need to be done for those activities.

❏ 8. Schedule them on your calendar and work your plan.

The steps in this chapter have led thousands of therapists to their dream practice - whether that was a boutique practice of five clients or a full practice of 30+. You can do it too.

WISDOM NUGGET

Being successful in private practice in these times is rarely by, 'luck of the draw.' It's about focusing, planning and having fun along the way. My thought is, "If it isn't fun, why bother?"

One of the best-kept secrets of the new practitioners who have built their practices quickly is, The Plan. When they think about marketing, these successful clinicians do not run for cover, nor do they run around in circles. They have a well conceived and consistently implemented Plan designed around their ideal client, and the therapist's own Marketing Personality Type.

Coaching Questions:

1. I often get a wide range of reactions when I share the marketing plan checklist. Some people get very excited as they now have a path to follow. Others feel overwhelmed and they aren't sure they want to do it. To address that, we go back to the current level of motivation. What does your private practice dream mean to you? What is your commitment level towards your dream, right now?

2. To build your marketing plan, I recommend you follow the steps in this chapter in order. If not, you're likely to waste a lot of time and maybe money too. If you find yourself wanting to jump in and skip the Vision or Ideal Client Exercises, why do you think that is? What will you benefit by skipping some steps?

3. When two or more work toward a goal, it can be more fun and have a higher chance of being accomplished. With whom could you share the process of building a marketing plan? This could be a family member who is helping you build your plan or a colleague who is building their plan – try using the checklist together.

CHAPTER THIRTY

17 Things You Can Do To Grow Your Practice

Here is an email I received recently:

"Casey, I have done everything I can think of to market my practice and nothing is working. I sent letters to physicians in my area. I took out an ad in the local paper, which cost $1000 (I only had enough money to run it once). I attend local therapist meetings and ask for referrals. Either I am doing something wrong or marketing just won't work for me. Thanks for listening. Michelle"

Yikes. I felt really bad for her. It seems she's right on both counts. What she's doing isn't going to work well and will cost her a lot of her hard-earned money.

In today's market, you'll need to spend some money to build a solid referral base and get clients - especially if you want those clients to be fee-for-service and not insurance clients. Accept that as a fact, and then invest your marketing dollars wisely.

WISDOM NUGGET

Referrals come from relationships - not from one-time ads or asking people you barely know. To build your practice, build relationships with your prospects and your referral sources.

Below is a list of several marketing activities you could use to connect with prospects and referrals sources. They can vary in price and effort. You may want to add some of your own to the list.

I like to think of this list as a buffet. Look at the items on the buffet. Walk around and see what is available before you gorge on something right away. Nibble a bit on a few by learning a little more about them.

Do not overflow your plate with all that you see. Your stomach and your head will hurt. Sample. Nibble. Look into some a little deeper. But do not expect to do them all because you will give yourself a heart attack. I mean it. Just review this list and see if there are two or three that look interesting to you. Then figure out what your three logical next steps are. As you begin to make some progress, you'll find the motivation and momentum to propel you forward.

Here are the specials on your marketing buffet menu:

1. Build Referral Partners Via Networking.

A referral partner is someone who offers non-competing services to your ideal client. Start first with who you know. Maybe you're on the PTA with a family law attorney or a massage therapist. These people may see potential clients in your specialty niche. Find out where potential referral partners hang out and get to know them. If you have a unique specialty (people with autism, people who've been victims of violent crime or preschoolers, etc.), share that with people at your therapist networking meetings. However, if you want the same client some other therapists want (a smart, motivated and wealthy woman who is upset that the decorator painted the walls bone white instead of eggshell) then consider spending more time with allied business professionals in business networking meetings such as Business Network International (BNI). Find potential referral partners you like and, over time, build relationships with them. As you know, quality relationships take time and effort but it's the quality of the relationship that will generate referrals.

2. Build Referral Partners in Other Ways.

Like Alani, you could volunteer your time for a charity where there are other volunteers who have connections with your target market. Let your passion show when you're with your children's teachers and your neighbors. Sprinkle in appropriate success stories and share your joy for your work. As people come to understand what you do, you will get referrals. But a lot of people have to know what you do.

3. Network With Prospects.

If you work with singles looking for a great life partner, visit a local singles event. As a mother with a specialty niche market of new mothers you'll want to attend any presentations in your area for moms, for example. Meet the other attendees. You will at some point be asked about yourself. Remember to always come from a, "How can I serve you?" place.

4. Speak.

Consider a "signature talk" or two designed to be of interest to your ideal client. Find organizations that service your ideal client and offer to do a presentation. Unless there is a spectacular reason not to, always speak for free. Don't lose a speaking opportunity because you asked for $500. If you speak for free and get one client, you're apt to make that $500 many times over. Make sure you have a way to keep in touch with the people that attended. New clients rarely sign up for therapy on the day you do a talk. You need to help them to know, like and trust you. Do this by offering a free report, audio or newsletter.

5. Use an Online Therapist Locator Service.

This is the best way to get an online presence if you don't have one yet. These are the new Yellow Pages. Make sure to get on at least two or three. Go to Google and type in whatever your client would be searching for: "find a therapist" or, "marriage counseling" – and your city. See which of these online therapist locators come up. Then sign up. If you worry about the cost, remember that one client coming for two or three sessions would pay for your listing for an entire year. See **www.BeAWealthyTherapist.com** for recommendations. My favorite is **www.Find-A-Therapist.com**. With that service, you can be on up to four of their sites for one annual fee. In my opinion this is a "must do" marketing strategy.

Here are some tips to improve your online therapist locator listing. Make sure your listing is 80% about the client and their pain and 20% about you. Be careful how many specialties you say you have. List more than five specialties and you will lose credibility.

Some people say their online therapist locator listing didn't work as they only got one or two clients a year. They forget to look at the amount of money they took in versus the amount of money the online therapist locator listing cost. Only in a couple of cases have I heard that people didn't get a very good return on this investment.

6. Create a Website.

Even if you think you don't, you need a website. You can get them very inexpensively and many hosting companies will offer easy templates for you to use. Make sure your website text is 80% about the client - the problem from their point of view and your hope for them. The remaining 20% can be about you - your story, credentials, etc. Design your website in a way that invites web visitors to come back to your site.

7. Blog.

A Blog is an inexpensive and easily 'update-able' website. You can put your newsletters on your Blog and invite others to comment. The search engines love Blogs as the content changes regularly. Consider posting a very short article (a paragraph or two) once a week on your Blog. If you can write an email, you can update a Blog. You may need some help getting started, but after that Blogs are very easy.

8. Consider Pay-Per-Click Advertising.

If you notice, when you search for something on Google, you will see some ads on the right and at the top called "Sponsored Listings." The owners of those businesses have agreed to pay Google a certain amount each time someone clicks on their ad. The business owner chooses the amount based on "search terms." If this appeals to you, visit **www.adwords.Google.com**. A note of caution: make sure you learn how to use pay-per-click advertising effectively or you can end up wasting a lot of money. If you do sign up, please spend the time and go through Google's tutorials. They are fabulous.

9. Try an Online Appointment Scheduler.

Imagine you need to find a therapist. You find one on the Internet and check out his website. You like what you see. It seems like the therapist understands your pain and wants to help. You look at the clock - it's 5:00 a.m. You know if you put a call in to this therapist, you probably won't receive a call back until after you have left for work. And you will be in a meeting all day. But wait. There is a button on the therapist's site that says, "Schedule An Appointment." You click on it and see the times that the therapist indicates he's available. You fill in your information, get an email confirmation and go into work relaxed - knowing you have an appointment for the following day.

These schedulers are a great way to get new clients and to reduce telephone tag when rescheduling with your existing clients. You set up what times you're willing to see people and you get an email whenever someone makes an appointment. They are password protected and the clients can see their own appointments, but no one else's.

Mark Saindon, an MFT in Portland Oregon use an online scheduler on his site at **www.MarkSaindon.com**. Mark says, "When I first considered using the online scheduler I was a bit skeptical about how it could help my business. Now, I wouldn't even *think* about being without it. Besides saving me phone time with my regular clients, who can now schedule their own appointments, there have been weeks where I have had up to five new referrals making appointments themselves through the online scheduler."

How cool is that?

10. Use Audio on Your Website.

Have a button where your web visitor can click and hear your voice. Welcome them to the site. Let them know you understand what it's like to be in pain. Let them know you want to help. But make it short and make it optional to listen to. An uninvited audio can scare people - especially when their speakers are turned up and they aren't expecting it. Has that ever happened to you? See the chapter "Top Banana Websites" for some great examples.

11. Ask Questions (the *Cosmo Quiz*) on Your Website.

When your website is targeted toward a particular niche specialty, it's a good idea to create a questionnaire with seven to ten questions on your site. They can help people determine if they need a therapist. Again, I suggest you check out the chapter, "Top Banana Websites" to find some excellent examples.

12. Try a New Business Card.

Does your business card let referral sources and prospective clients understand whom you help? Does it stand out among the other therapist cards? Make sure your business card is a quality card. Don't use free business card services. Also, your business card is one of your most important marketing tools. Don't put your appointment card on the back of it. Imagine - you give your card to a referral source, they flip it over to write a note about you, and it has an appointment card on the back. Imagine - one of your clients wants to refer you to her business colleague - she hands out a copy of your card to the colleague and realizes with horror, that her next appointment time with you is on the back.

    Please be sure to stay away from the "free" business card printers on the Internet. First, you don't want to have a flimsy business card. You want to look very professional. Second, you may pick a design that many other therapists have and it'll look like you all work in the same practice. Whenever I speak, I can guarantee that I will get between two and four therapists handing me identical looking business cards - an ocean scene – and I know these therapists don't even know each other.

13. Offer Tip Sheets.

People love free stuff. Have a "Tip Sheet" you give away: "5 Things To Do When You Feel the Blues Coming On." Or, "The 8 Biggest Mistakes New Step-Moms Make and How You Can Avoid Them." Or, "10 Tips for Couples Marrying for the Second Time." You get the idea. Make it something your ideal client would love. (Remember the ideal client you created as the second step of your *Marketing Plan Checklist?* Have another conversation with that fictitious, ideal client about what they would like to read).

14. Write Articles.

Write five articles and submit them in a packet to your weekly community paper and offer to do a column for them. Consider writing articles and submitting them to newsletters or publications that your ideal client reads. This may not bring in a zillion clients, but it'll give you some prestige and help set you apart as "an expert." If you read a story in your local paper and you have some expertise in that area, call the author or editor and ask if they'd like your take on the story. They may consider you as a resource to quote in the future.

15. Podcast.

A Podcast is an online radio show that you create in the same way you might create an audio recording. You record something with an introduction and a closing, then put it on your website or upload it to a Podcasting service like iTunes. Then the general public checks out what Podcasts are available and they can "subscribe" to ones that strike their fancy. The subscribers will then be notified whenever you create a new show. In a way, you could think of it as an audio newsletter, only much cooler.

Sheri Zampelli, Hypnotherapist, coach and owner of **www.DonateYourWeight.com** uses Podcasting as one of her primary marketing strategies. Donate Your Weight is a program based on Seven Stress-Free Slimming Strategies™. She helps people undo all that created their weight problem, while teaching them new behaviors that will lead to lifetime results without diets, pills, shots, surgery or struggle. Sheri says, "Podcasting has been a great way for me to reach a worldwide audience. It has resulted in CD sales, coaching clients, Teleseminar attendees and it has helped me to make beneficial business contacts with ease. I plan to use the recorded content in the future as part of my product line. I notice that when I talk to someone who is a Podcast listener, I do not have to sell him or her on my products or services, they are pre-sold because they've been listening to the show and they already know what I'm all about. On average 1,000 - 1,300 people are downloading the show each week and the numbers have been steadily rising all year long."

16. Record a Message.

Don't feel like creating a Podcast? You can create a short message on a phone answering machine offering hope and help. Then put that number on your website or in any print advertising. For example,

"Call xxx-xxxx if you are looking for tips on how to find your special mate. Listen anytime 24/7 to a pre-recorded message that may help you stop 'looking for love in all the wrong places'." Of course you need to make sure it is ethical and appropriate, but a recorded message can offer a potential client a way to get a sense of you before they call for an appointment. Please make sure this is on a separate telephone line - not your outgoing office voicemail message.

17. Use Direct Mail.

Direct mail means sending a letter or postcard to potential clients. Some therapists buy a list of qualified prospects from a "list service" and then send letters out to them. If you have a very good list, and a well-defined specialty niche, this can be effective. Sometimes, though, it can end up costing more money and effort than it's worth. Should you decide to do direct mail, know that you can probably expect 0.5% to 1.5% of the people receiving the marketing piece to show some interest. And usually this is on a marketing piece that's sent out at least three times. Again, this can be an effective strategy but, as with pay-per-click advertising, proceed with caution and monitor your results carefully.

So how are you doing? I know there is a lot of information here. My goal is to help you see that there are lots of options. Some you will like more than others and some will be easier for you. Go with your strengths. Do what seems the most interesting or the most fun. Make a plan, but don't make it drudgery. Most of my clients tell me that at first they disliked marketing, but they came to enjoy it quite a bit when they learned what to do and how to do it. Please remember Richard Dreyfuss's advice in the hilarious movie, *What About Bob?* Each week make "baby steps." Pretty soon you will see results.

If you're like Michelle and have tried a lot of things that didn't work, then spend some time figuring out why they may not have worked. For example, Michelle paid $1000 for an ad to run once. The ad was lost among many other ads. I'd bet the farm that her ad said something about counseling rather than addressing the problem from her ideal client's point of view. Imagine if she had spent that money on an annual subscription to two online therapist locator listings and BNI networking dues for a year. How much better might that have worked out for her?

I know you can do this. Just do not bite off more than you can chew. Check out the Marketing Buffet list.

Then consider what two or three marketing activities might work best with your Marketing Personality Type.

To help you with that, we have a chart in the next chapter.

Warning - Shameless Plug: I have found that this amount of information is difficult to absorb in one sitting. If you'd like more detailed instructions on these marketing activities, you may want to consider the *Be A Wealthy Therapist Implementation Kit*. It consists of twelve audio CDs and a 130-page workbook manual called, *How To Build Your Full and Rewarding Private Practice*. You can read more about it and get your special discount at: **www.BeAWealthyTherapist.com/bookreadersonly/**

There is also more information about it, and other resources in the back of this book.

Now, let's match the marketing activities with the Four Marketing Personality Types.

Coaching Questions:

1. List the marketing efforts you have tried in the past. What results did you have for each? Why do you think you had those results?

2. What is your reaction to this Marketing Buffet list of activities to grow your practice? Are you feeling a little scared or hopeful? Which two or three strike you as interesting or fun? Are you willing to try those? If so, what do you see as your three next steps to make it work?

3. Who might you review this list with as you think about what would work best for you?

CHAPTER THIRTY-ONE

Match Your Marketing Personality Type

Years ago, I visited a traditional Polish Catholic family that went out for "fish-fry" every Friday. Not being very fond of fish (especially deep-fried), I assumed I could skip the fish and eat the green salad and vegetables. The 'salad' was runny cottage cheese. Not a vegetable in sight.

The matriarch of the family kept heaping cottage cheese on my plate. I like cottage cheese less than fish, (truth be told, it makes me very ill), so I wasn't going to eat it either. I stuck to my guns and politely sipped my ice tea. I got a lot of disapproving looks.

That night, all eight members of the family came down with very bad food poisoning, but I was fine. The moral of the story - you don't have to eat cottage cheese (or fish) if you hate it. And it's really a good idea not to.

The same is true in marketing. If you cannot stand speaking, then don't plan on giving presentations. Don't put that much pressure on yourself. Pick another activity that's more suited to you. (Although, if you're just a little nervous about speaking, please see the chapter "Do I Have To Give Presentations?" It may lessen your anxiety).

Below is a chart that shows which marketing activities work with the Four Marketing Personality Types. Take a glance and see if there are a few you'd like to consider.

Activity	Extrovert	Introvert	Techno Lover	Creative
Build Referral Partners Via Networking	X	X		X
Build Referral Partners in Other Ways	X	X		X
Network with Prospects	X	X		X
Speaking	X	X		X
Online Therapist Locator Service	X	X	X	X
Website	X	X	X	X
Blog		X	X	X
Pay-Per-Click Advertising		X	X	
Online Appointment Scheduler		X	X	
Audio on the Website	X	X	X	X
Assessment (the Cosmo Quiz) on Your Website	X	X	X	X
New Business Card	X	X	X	X
Tip Sheet	X	X	X	X
Write Articles		X	X	X
Podcasting		X	X	X
Record a Message		X	X	
Direct Mail (it may or may not work - depending on your market)		?		?

You may not agree with what I have indicated here. For example, not every Introvert will feel comfortable networking, but some might if they attended a BNI meeting. BNI meetings are very structured and can make most introverts feel at ease.

This chart isn't meant to be the "final word" on what will work for you. It's included to give you some ideas. But like I said, only sample what you think you might enjoy - although, I invite you to stretch yourself on occasion. But like yoga, do it at your own pace and "breathe" into the stretch.

Coaching Questions:

1. What three activities will you commit to learn more about?

2. When picking a new marketing activity, it's always a good idea to set a goal. For example, "I will visit two networking meetings before deciding which one to join." Or, "I will put an online scheduler on my website within three weeks." What might your goal be?

3. Who might you share this list with? Who would be a good person to help you sort through the options?

CHAPTER THIRTY-TWO

Do Letters Work?

I hear this a lot:

"Marketing does not work for me. I sent out letters to several physicians and I never got a single referral from them."

I used to say it a lot too.

Once, I sent out 100 letters to veterinarians in my area explaining that I like to help people with "Pet Loss." I filled the letters with "one free session" cards for the vet staff to give people who are grief-struck because they have had to put down a beloved pet.

I told my assistant Kathy to be ready. Even if only ten of them sent me two referrals each, I should have at least twenty new clients within a few weeks. My caseload would be very full, so I asked Kathy to let me know when I needed to open up some additional appointment times to accommodate all these new clients. We made a dozen new client intake packets.

I got three calls.

One was from a vet who wanted to point out to me that the initials after his name should have been D.V.M. - Doctor of Veterinary Medicine. He was very, very upset because I had mistakenly put the initials as D.M.V. - as in, *Department of Motor Vehicles.* (I was mortified at first, and then thought it was wildly funny.)

The second call came from a woman who had just lost her Siberian Husky. This dog was more like a child than her pet. I spoke to her on the phone on a Friday night for 30 minutes trying to calm her. We finally scheduled an appointment for Monday. She called Monday morning and cancelled the appointment as she, "was doing so much better that she went out over the weekend and bought a new puppy." (I know many people have done well with the Pet Loss niche - I just wasn't one of them.)

The third call came from a vet who asked me to do some team building with his staff. They were a great bunch of people, but after two sessions, it was over.

Kathy and I were very confused. This should have been a slam-dunk way to fill the practice. We sent out 100 letters.

We were talking about this as I was opening my mail.

In the mail was a letter from a therapist announcing that her practice was opening in my area. She gave all of her credentials, affiliations, and publications. She wrote that she worked with anxiety, depression, OCD, PTSD, relationships, anger, thought disorders, personality disorders, grief and loss, death and dying, Christians, gays, lesbians, bisexuals and transgenders and, of course, she did pre-marital, marital, divorce and separation work. She gave her address and phone number and ended the letter with, "I would really appreciate your referrals." Inside the envelope were five business cards.

Kathy and I were still trying to figure out why my phone wasn't ringing off the hook as I threw away this therapist's letter and her cards. Kathy asked why I was trashing the letter.

"I don't know this person. How could I give them any referrals?"

It was like in the cartoons when the light bulb goes off over the characters heads. Instantly, we both got it.

Case Study:
A caring therapist shows how much he cares.

My colleague, David Kuroda (the LCSW I wrote about earlier), doesn't write bulk letters and send them out to people he doesn't know. However he does send cards and notes that result in new referrals to his practice. In fact, this is an important way he markets his practice.

For example, when David hears that one of the lawyers he knows has suffered a loss, he acknowledges it with a card and expressions of sympathy. He tells this story: "Once I went to a dinner where an attorney was honored. At the dinner, I made a point of speaking with her and meeting her husband. A while later, I heard her husband had died. I sent her a note telling her how sorry I was for her loss. I told her that it was great that her husband had had the opportunity to see her recognized at that event. A year later, two very high profile cases came my way from that attorney."

By allowing the attorney to see that he really cares about people, David is showing the quality of his character. He's showing her how thoughtful he is. He becomes memorable to her.

David also regularly sends articles to people he knows. For example, if he finds an interesting article on children and divorce, he will send it with a personal note to a family court judge he knows. In the note, he'll say, "You may not have seen this and I thought it might be of interest to you." Then he writes, "I appreciate the work you're doing." He doesn't usually include a business card. That way, it comes across as David wanting to share his resources with others rather than asking for referrals. In doing this, he builds relationships. People see his character and want to refer to him.

WISDOM NUGGET

Referrals come from building relationships with your prospects and your referral sources - not from letters sent to people you don't know.

People will hire you as their therapist or give you referrals when they:

1. *Know you.*
2. *Like you.*
3. *Trust you.*
4. *Believe you have the solution to their problem.*
5. *Are ready.*

Your job is to show you care - that you understand the problems they struggle with - so that, when they are ready, yours is the phone number they dial.

Coaching Questions:

1. What marketing efforts have you tried that just did not work as you expected?

2. Where do your referrals come from now?

3. Consider connecting with a colleague to laugh over what did not work. (Let's never take ourselves too seriously.) Come up with some new ideas that might help prospects get to know, like and trust you.

CHAPTER THIRTY-THREE

Do I Have to Give Presentations?

If you were asked to give a presentation in front of a roomful of your prospective, ideal clients, how would you go about it? Would you feel like you needed to do some more research? Would you write out your talk ahead of time in order not to forget anything? Do you see yourself as relaxed or a bit anxious when preparing and when presenting?

What would you imagine the audience wants from you? Think about that for a moment. *What would they want from you?* What would make them feel comfortable? What would make them feel like it was an interesting event to attend? When people feel that you listen to them and validate their points, they like you and want more of what you have to offer. Instead of giving a lecture with a dozen points, consider presenting a few points and get a discussion going. A good facilitator is often much more interesting than a lecturer.

Case Study: "The Dad's Coach"

Mark Hastings, an MFT and coach in Pasadena, California is known as, "The Dad's Coach." Mark helps "good dads become great dads." There is a new breed of young fathers that want to hear his message, but Mark was nervous about the marketing activity of giving presentations. He was worried that he didn't have enough content and he was wondering how to keep the men interested during the entire talk.

When Mark was able to reframe "giving a presentation" to, "facilitating a group discussion," his anxiety reduced significantly. He realized that some content was needed, but too much content might be off-putting.

Mark has developed several talks now and they all have a similar format. He joins with the audience in the beginning. He asks three questions (or variations of these three questions) and then facilitates the discussion. He sprinkles in his points and knowledge as he creates a lively discussion. He has been so successful that he has been getting requests from groups asking for additional presentations.

One presentation Mark gave was to a group of dads at a local church. It was called, "Five Tips for Raising Great, Responsible Kids in a Media-Saturated Society." After joining with them, his first question to the group was, "Do you think it's hard to raise great, responsible kids in today's media-saturated society - where our seven-year-old daughters want to look and act like Brittany Spears?" Now that gets the men talking. They talked about their concerns and Mark facilitated smoothly: "Great answer - who else has a thought on that?"

Then Mark asked, "What have you tried that didn't seem to make a difference? Does shutting off the TV work?" An interesting discussion ensued with Mark sharing his ideas too.

Finally, the audience is asked, "What does work? What can we do to make sure our children have the values we want and not the cultural values that the media portrays?" This is where Mark will share his list of three or four ideas if the group doesn't. But often, they do and Mark again *facilitates* the discussion, adding his professional input where appropriate.

At the end, Mark has a feedback form. On the form, the audience has the opportunity to request a copy of one of Mark's articles. His most requested article is, "Of Michelins and Men" - a great story about dads, tires and priorities. He then sends this article to those requesting it - thanking them for their warm welcome and saying, "If I can serve you in any way, please let me know."

Imagine giving yourself permission to join with the audience in a warm way where you talk only about half the time. Imagine that you're facilitating rather than reading or reciting a talk you have memorized. Imagine how your audience would feel as you connected with them. Instead of glazed-over expressions, you see people anxious to connect with you and the rest of the group.

Mark still gives great content and the audience feels connected with him. And his phone is ringing.

Oh, and by the way, speaking isn't Mark's only marketing activity. He has a listing on www.Counsel-Search.com and they also host his website: **www.TheDadsCoach.com** Check it out. The website text is a great example of explaining what he does by connecting with the problem from his ideal client's perspective. You can also read the article, "Of Michelins and Men" on his site.

W I S D O M   N U G G E T

Wisdom nugget: You don't need to do more research. To be successful at giving a presentation, simply have a few points and connect with your audience. While it's called, "speaking," I like to think of it as "listening" as much as speaking.

Imagine yourself in front of the audience and facilitating a group discussion rather than giving a dry lecture with questions at the end. See yourself interacting just as you might if you were leading a group therapy session. Notice that those in attendance are actively participating as you lead them with some interesting questions. They love you. Make sure you offer them the opportunity for more from you, with your feedback form.

Coaching Questions:

1. On a scale of 1 to 10, where 1 is suicidal and 10 is super-confident, where was your anxiety level at the thought of speaking in front of a group, before you read Mark's story? After reading it, have you noticed any change in your discomfort?

2. What happens to you when you imagine yourself *facilitating* a presentation this way?

3. Is there a colleague with whom you could discuss this idea further and look for ways you could modify it to match your style and implement it in your marketing plan?

CHAPTER THIRTY-FOUR

Network With the World's Largest Referral Organization

As an introvert who gets sweaty palms at the thought of talking to anyone new, when someone suggested, "build your practice by joining a business networking meeting", I freaked. So I did what all introverted therapists do when presented with something they are uncomfortable with - I took a class. Then I took more classes.

I have actually taken five different classes on, "How to Be Successful at Networking." I hoped it would be kind of like "*in vivo* desensitization." I thought the more classes I took, the less scared I would be. But, learning how to fly in a plane from the comfort of a classroom is not the same as being 30,000 feet in the air, as anyone with a flying phobia will tell you.

So, I called several business networking referral groups and attended two as a visitor. (These meetings are often listed in the Business section of the newspaper. In many areas they are published on Mondays.)

It turned out to be nowhere near as scary as I had imagined. People were kind and welcoming. There was a structured agenda that helped me a great deal.

Years later, I kept hearing about BNI - Business Network International. I visited and became a member and later, a director. In my opinion, BNI is one of the best referral organizations there is. I recommend it highly.

In case you haven't heard of BNI, it's the world's largest referral organization. In fact BNI has more members than all the other word-of-mouth referral organizations combined. As of 2006, BNI had 4800 chapters in 37 countries. Referrals among those members produced $2 billion for BNI members. Today there are over 100,000 BNI members. Statistically, the average BNI member increases their business by $30,000 - all that for an annual investment of under $400. That seems like a great return on investment to me.

Many, many therapists I have coached have become active BNI members and received three to ten clients a year from BNI referrals - some have even received more than that. At first blush this might not seem like a lot of referrals, but what does an average client spend with you? This means your BNI referral income can run into the thousands. And don't forget that those clients will tell others and you will have more referrals.

One thing I love about BNI is that no matter where you are – in another city or another country, the meeting agenda is exactly the same. You can attend a BNI meeting anywhere the world and except for the language, it'll look exactly like your local meeting. They have discovered a format that works, and they stick to it.

Why do I mention that? I don't expect that you will be getting referrals from around the world. But, for an introvert, knowing the meeting will have the same format each week is comforting. I know what to expect.

WISDOM NUGGET:

Maybe you aren't familiar with business networking referral groups. It's a group of business professionals who meet on a weekly basis to support each other's businesses and share information and referrals. There is one person per occupation - one financial planner, one personal trainer, one real estate agent. You get the idea. They act as a sales force for each other's businesses.

I was in a group with a decorative cake maker. When I heard someone talking about a special occasion, I asked if they needed a cake. If so, I referred them to Marian who made everything from multi-tier wedding cakes to cartoon cakes for the kids. People were grateful for the referral.

"But business networking or referral organizations are unethical and I can't imagine how you could in good faith recommend them for therapists," one therapist said to me after I did a presentation on practice building. As with any advice in this book, please make sure you're complying with the ethical and legal requirements of your license type.

For me, it's wonderful when I can refer a family member, colleague or even a client of mine to someone that I know, like and trust. You don't ever have to refer clients to anyone in the group if that makes you feel uncomfortable.

But what about that? What do you think about referring a client to someone in your networking group? Again, check out what is legal and ethical. But many therapists see providing resources to their clients as a service. Most of us do it all the time anyway. We refer to attorneys, doctors, and other ancillary service providers. You know your clients. You know where it would be helpful and appropriate and where it wouldn't. Some therapists choose to never refer their clients to anyone in the group. That's fine - it's your choice. But if I was your client and you had a good referral to a massage therapist or printer, I'd like that referral. Of course, I never make a referral to anyone that I don't feel comfortable with - even if they are in a group with me. Either I have worked with that person, or know people who have and have been pleased.

For more information on BNI, visit their website at www.bni. com and get the names of the directors in your area. Ask them if there is a chapter opening for a therapist in your area.

W I S D O M   N U G G E T

Some clinicians report, "networking doesn't work." When I explore it with them, they usually tell me they come late, leave early and never meet with anyone outside the group. By the way, I tried that for a while and they are right – using that strategy, networking will not work.

How can you be more successful at networking? Here are my recommendations:

1. Pick a group that you like - where the other members might be people who also serve your target market. Take advantage of all the education they offer. BNI offers its members over 100,000 hours of training a year. If networking isn't working, as you'd like - get a mentor and attend the trainings.

2. As always, talk about what you do and whom you serve in a way that the members can really understand.

3. Meet with members outside of the meeting to get to know, like and trust them and help them to do the same with you. (This is one of the best marketing strategies for therapists - you can connect with these referral sources one-on-one just like you do in your work.)

4. Educate the members on how to give you a referral. Most other people don't know how to politely refer someone to a therapist. In order to get referrals from your group, you must teach them how to make a referral to you. Give them the words to use.

5. Be careful that you don't go broke buying services from the other members. It's great to support your chapter, but if everyone just buys each other's service, the chapter won't make it. Get to know people and find out who is a good referral for them. Keep your eyes and ears open for someone who may need their services then, if appropriate, make the referral.

Networking isn't just for extroverts.

Check out a local BNI chapter. Even introverts can feel very comfortable there. Get to know the people. Teach them how to give a referral to you.

Know that it's about wanting to give other people referrals as well - don't join just to get them.

Coaching Questions:

1. Have you been to a business-networking meeting where referrals to the group members were passed? Have you been to a BNI meeting? If so, what type of success did you see among the group members?

2. Can you see how BNI could work for the Introverted Marketing Personality Type if the therapist was willing to spend time with the members of the group?

3. What might your next steps be?

CHAPTER THIRTY-FIVE

Attract Attention With Articles

A very cost effective method to get the word out about your practice is to write articles for publication. You can write for print publications or for the Internet. Whether online or offline, being an author helps you gain credibility and reminds people how to get in touch with you. As you write with your ideal client in mind, you will find that your audience feels they come to know you. Think of some of the columnists you read regularly. Doesn't it feel like you know them? That sense of connection can help you build a relationship with your readers. And, again, referrals come from recognition and from relationships.

My tips for using articles to position yourself as an expert:

1. Focus on your specialty niche. Give the readers tips, strategies and ideas about how to solve their problems. Sometimes well-meaning professionals write articles about too many different topics and their credibility is compromised. If you present yourself as master of a zillion things, you may be seen as a master of none.

2. Once you get a rhythm going, write several articles at a time. Your articles don't have to be long - maybe 500 words - on various questions and concerns that your clients have. If you write several at a time, you can do so when your energy and creativity are flowing. This means you have several articles for

distribution. You really look like the expert.

3. How are you going to distribute your articles? You can either submit them to offline (print) publications or online (web-based distribution services). As noted earlier, you can send a series of five to a local publication and suggest that you do a column for them - with the articles you send as a sample. Send them to former clients or current prospects. You could send them once a month to people you think have the problem that you'd like to help them solve. Ask your referral sources if they'd like some copies for their office lobbies. What about online distribution? All over the web, there are electronic magazines (called ezines) that cover many issues and topics. There are also distribution companies that will take your submitted article and, for free or for a small fee, distribute them to hundreds of ezine publishers. For more information, check out **www.EzineArticles.com.**

4. At the end of every article published, there is a "resource box" about the author. This contains your contact information and the answer to the question, "So what do you do for a living?" In the resource box, have a call to action. Invite the reader to further the relationship with you. For example, "Call today for your free initial consultation." Or, "Email today to get your free copy of our special report, 'Top 10 Ways to (fill in your specialty here)'."

5. Make sure your article title is fun, upbeat and has a unique twist. The purpose of the title (or headline) is to get them to read the first sentence. Make sure your title is something that would draw your reader to want to know more. People like titles with numbers as you can see by some of these best sellers: "The Five Love Languages", "Seven Habits of Highly

Effective People," and "1000 Places to See Before You Die."
It makes you want to read more to see what the tips are.

6. Ask all publishers to send you a copy of the article. If possible, ask them if you can review the resource box prior to publication to make sure it's to your liking.

Do you have a book in you? These days it's not all that difficult to write a book and self-publish it or have it published by a small publishing house. Unless you write a best seller, your book is probably not going to make you a lot of money. But it'll open doors for you in surprising ways.

WISDOM NUGGET

We all have short memories. It takes people five to nine times to hear of you before they decide to hire you. Don't just write one article, but several, about something of interest to your ideal client. Then create your article distribution plan.

Editors are often looking for content for their magazines or newspapers. Also, distribute your articles to your network. Articles alone probably won't fill your practice, but as you gain credibility with articles and your other marketing efforts, more clients should be calling you. To get started, pick a topic that would be of interest to your niche market and put quill to parchment.

Coaching Questions:

1. Back to your fictitious ideal client, what would she or he find interesting and want to read about?

2. Is writing something you enjoy? If not, consider recording your thoughts and creating "audio articles" for your web visitors to listen to.

3. If writing is something you enjoy, what might your next steps be to explore this?

CHAPTER THIRTY-SIX

Top Banana Websites

Face it - we are all curious. When we hear of a new movie or a new book, many of us go to the web to check it out.

WISDOM NUGGET

These days, people who hear about you will want to check you out before they call. They will probably Google you. An Internet presence is no longer really an option if you want a full practice. You must have an online presence with either a great online therapist locator listing, a website or a Blog in order to have people consider you a "real business."

A great website does two things:

1. It helps people get a sense of you - what you're all about - not just a series of credentials.

2. It invites the web visitor to take the next step - get a special report or take an assessment. Then it makes it easy for them to make an appointment.

Let's look at how some therapists use their website to do this.

Case Study:
Online Marketing Builds a Practice in Six Months.

Roberta Wands, MFT, practices in Riverside, California. Roberta was licensed in November 2005 and started her practice in January 2006. Roberta has put in place such an excellent online marketing plan that she told me, "Within six months of starting my practice, it was taking off and has been doing really well since. In fact, as of January 2007, I have not done anything new to market my practice. No new marketing time at all!! Zero. And my income has doubled this year."

She credits her incredible success to:

- Creating a specialized practice.
- Using her website to speak to the main problem her potential ideal clients are currently experiencing.
- Advertising on online therapist locators such as, "Psychology Today" and "Counsel-Search," and sending out a newsletter through "Constant Contact."

These are the only marketing activities Roberta does. Her entire marketing strategy is done via the Internet. No networking meetings to attend. No speaking engagements to acquire.

Roberta's specialty is helping people in difficult relationships decide whether to stay and improve the relationship or leave it. Her website is called **www.MakeUpOrBreakUpCounseling.com**. The colors are a soft blue and white and visually, this is a very soothing site.

Let's look at three things that make this a great website to visit and why it's so successful for Roberta.

1. The headline speaks directly to her ideal client's pain and to the hope she has for them: "Are You Facing the Possibility of a Marriage Breakup? Discover How You Can Turn Your Marriage Around - And Just Maybe, Prevent Your Divorce!" Wow. That makes me keep reading.

2. On the left, she has a short audio that welcomes you to her site. Her voice sounds quite soothing. As you listen, you clearly get the sense that she understands the pain of facing a breakup. (She even says she was once there too - so she totally gets it.) "But there is good news!" she tells us. She tells her web visitors exactly what to do next. She tells them how to navigate her site and how to connect with her. She doesn't read a long phone number over the recording. She asks the web visitor: "So would you like to get started right away? Scroll down and take our free quiz: 'Is your relationship in trouble?' It'll help you discover if your relationship needs immediate help. Then go to the "Contact Me" page on this site

and you can sign up for a free 15-minute consultation with me."

3. On the right, Roberta offers a Free Special Report: "3 Simple Secrets To Help Get Your Marriage Back On Track, Today!" This report is sent immediately via email. People can read more about Roberta's wisdom and get even more of a sense of her.

This website is very "client attractive." It not only touches people's emotions and shows she cares; it also guides people to the next step of getting help. Rock on Roberta.

Case Study #2: Be Yourself.

If you look in the dictionary under, "Creative Marketing Personality Type," you should see Judy Westerfield's picture. Judy is an MFT in Orange County, California who has broadened her scope from traditional psychotherapy and hypnosis to offer retreats, workshops, CEU programs and "days of play."

Judy's first love and best friend is Max - her part-Terrier, part-Basset dog. Judy credits Max as being the "most quirky, creative and healing creature" she knows and her website is dedicated to him. Judy's website is **www.CreativityToTheMax.com**

I want you to see Judy's website because it isn't a traditional therapist website. It's whimsical and playful. The colors are a bright blue with playful icons at the top that direct you to various pages. You immediately get the sense that Judy doesn't take herself (or life) too seriously. Which is interesting as she lives with chronic pain and many of her programs are designed for people living with chronic pain. She offers other programs as well. For example, CEU programs for therapists. In these workshops, she teaches clinicians how to tap into their own creativity and to use creativity with their clients. And as you can see on her site, the workshops have really enticing titles such as, Celebrating Your Inner Diva.

Judy's website has an online registration feature where people can sign up easily for her workshops. This eliminates a lot of the telephone tag and makes it convenient for the registrant. There is also some fun free stuff on her site such as, "Creative Journaling Tips for Beginners." And if you have some fun pet peeves, you can email them to Max - in care of Judy because apparently Judy has not given Max his own computer - yet.

As I look at this site and write this, I find myself smiling. That's exactly what Judy wants her web visitor to do when they visit. This is a happy site. I love it.

Case Study #3:
Nancy's Counseling Corner.

"Relationships. We all want them and need them. How to get them and keep them." This is the beginning of the welcome message on Nancy Travers' website, **www.NancysCounselingCorner.com.** Nancy is an LCSW in Irvine, California and she has created a pretty website with a cute logo and a mixture of pretty purple colors.

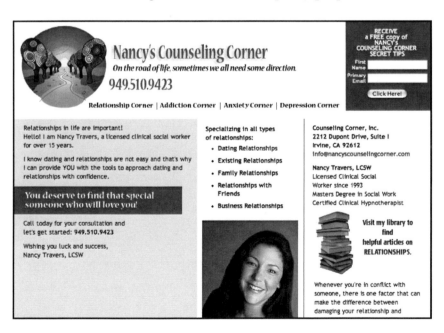

When you visit this site you see Nancy's smiling face. Under her picture, you can click a link to hear the welcome message. In the top right, she has a sign-up box where you can get a free copy of her "Secret Tips."

When you click on her navigational tabs, such as "Relationship Corner," you will be presented with a simple example of what I call the "The Cosmo Quiz" assessment. There are a series of questions and Nancy says, "If you answered yes to EVEN ONE QUESTION, you might benefit from the support and strategies of a counselor." Then she writes, "You don't have to go through this alone" and gives her phone number and invites the web visitor to call for an appointment.

This site clearly shows Nancy's personality - caring and to the point. It makes great use of the various marketing features we have discussed. It helps people who have heard about Nancy get a better sense of her personality and what she has to offer. Great site, Nancy.

Case Study #4:
The Divorce Coach

To hear a fabulous welcome audio, please visit Susie Duffy's site **www.DivorceCoach.org** Her voice is confident and her message really gets at the heart of her ideal client's struggle. This is one of the best introductory audios I have ever heard on a website.

This website is soothing and makes one want to read more. On this site you will also see a great example of an interactive quiz. The web visitor is invited to answer some questions. Through some programming, the quiz is scored. Based on how they score, one of three responses is sent to the web visitor inviting them to take the next step to get some support. This is a great way to connect way with your web visitor. Terrific site, Susie.

I am grateful to these clinicians for allowing me to showcase their sites. As you can see, they are all very different and all appealing to different types of clients. Roberta created her site herself using resources at **www.Homestead.com** while Judy, Nancy, and Susie created the content and hired web designers to do the technical work.

With your site, allow your personality to come through. Show the reader you care. Make it easy for them to connect with you.

Top Banana websites have six things in common.

1. *They speak about what they do in ways that their ideal client would appreciate.*
2. *They offer something for free.*
3. *They have a clear "call to action" and they make it easy to contact them.*
4. *They reflect the personality and display a picture of the therapist.*
5. *They spend at least 80% of the site geared toward their ideal client.*
6. *They are simple. To the point. Caring.*

Coaching Questions:

1. Take a look at these sites and a few other therapist's websites. Imagine you're a person who is searching for a therapist. What appeals to you? What do you need to read that would compel you to pick up the phone and call one of these therapists rather than look for one on your insurance panel?

2. Does the idea of creating an online marketing strategy seem like a good option for you? Why or why not?

3. Consider pairing up with a friend and looking at various websites. Create a list of all the things you like and don't like about their sites. For those sites you like, consider contacting the therapist and ask who did their site and how it's working for them. Most therapists who have created an online marketing strategy are happy to share their experiences with others.

CHAPTER THIRTY-SEVEN

What About Blogs?

When I was trying to explain what a Blog was to my aged mother-in-law Ann, she put it very well. She said, "That's interesting. But everything is so complicated these days."

There is a saying that goes like this: 'Technology is what happened after you were born. And if it happened after you were born, it seems complicated.' To my mother-in-law, a microwave is "technology", but her granddaughter would never think so. You and I probably don't think of television as "technology," but "high definition, Blu-Ray discs" may seem like "technology" to us.

But there is some great news. As technology advances, it actually becomes easier for the at-home user to take advantage of. Let me explain.

In 1975 I graduated with a degree in Computer Science from SUNY. To put things in perspective, the computer that ran the entire college was stored in a huge building covering an entire city block. That same computer can now fit on a tiny thumb-size flash drive. The computer inside a simple iPod today has over 80 times the storage space of my entire college computer in 1975. There were no personal computers then. Now, most children aged five to eight can navigate their home computer easily.

So, why can a five-year-old do it so easily? Because many programs have been designed with the end user (aka: you) in mind. While they take a bit of instruction, they are easy to use.

A website use to be a $20,000 project. And every time you wanted to update your website you had to hire the designer to make changes which added to the cost.

Now we have Weblogs or Blogs. A Blog is an easily update-able website. If you write an email, you can update a Blog. Some therapists are now using a Blog as their primary website. It allows the clinician to easily add or change content. While you may need some help getting set up, if you can write an email, you can update your Blog.

Case Study:

My friend, Maria Xanthos, is an MFT in Fullerton, California. Maria has had a very successful general practice for about 20 years. Maria is well known in local medical circles and gets many of her referrals from physicians. She recently decided to add a specialization of helping people through the divorce process. She needed an online presence and wanted it up quickly.

We found a place to host her site. Amber, my amazing right hand, created a Blog for Maria at **www.YourDivorceCoach.com**. In less than one day, Maria's Blog was up and running. Here is a picture of our first draft:

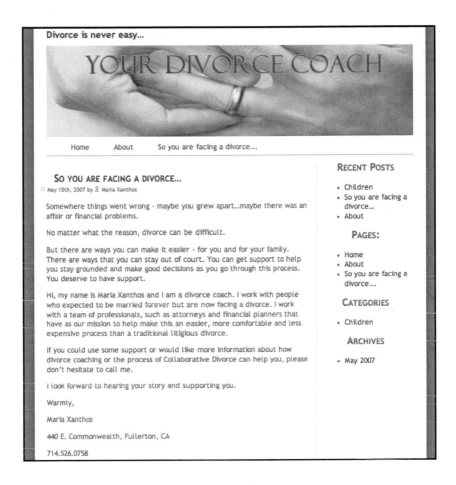

We certainly may revise this over time and may create a website too. But for now, this is a great way for people to connect with Maria and get an initial sense of her.

W ISDOM NUGGET

If entering the world of technology feels daunting to you, please consider it anyway. There are so many easy things you can do. As you saw with many of the case studies, it'll be a very important marketing strategy in the future.

You can not only use a Blog as your website, you can also use it to create community. For your next group or workshop, you can create a new Blog and invite the participants to connect with each other via comments on the Blog. You can post any homework assignments or handouts easily on a Blog. You can read our, Be A Wealthy Therapist newsletters at our Blog at:
www.BeAWealthyTherapist.com/Blog/

Coaching Questions:

1. Do you read any Blogs now? Do you know any people who use their Blog as their website?

2. How do you feel about using technology in general? How can you use technology in your marketing plan?

3. Explore some Blogs. In fact, feel free to visit my Blog and let me know what you think of the book. You can leave me a comment at: **www.BuildYourTherapyPractice.com/bookcomment**

CHAPTER THIRTY-EIGHT

The Importance of Keeping in Touch

There is an old adage in marketing that goes like this: a person often needs to hear about you at least five to nine times before they buy from you. How does this relate to therapists?

We are in the business of providing psychotherapy services. People often think about going to therapy long before they finally call for an appointment. They may have heard of a great therapist that helped some friends. A doctor may have made a referral. They may have attended a community lecture years ago and they liked the speaker/therapist. Who do they finally call when they are ready?

There is another marketing expression called "top of mind." This is who they will call – the person whose name is in the "top of (their) mind" - when they are finally ready to schedule an appointment. So your goal is to be "top of mind." This is why it's important to follow through and continue to stay in touch with prospects. You want to be "top of mind" when they decide they are ready.

The way to do this is to develop a good contact management system and have a system for keeping in touch with prospects and referral partners. A contact management system can be a manual system (rolodex and index cards) or a computer program that has an automated address book. There are many good ones on the market.

Simply put, you want to keep track of each person who shows an interest in what you offer. Then you develop a "keep in touch" strategy to contact them at regular intervals. This contact may be in the form of a newsletter, a handwritten note, an invitation to a free lecture or class or a telephone call. In your contact management system, you note the *last* contact and plan ahead for the *next* contact with that prospect or referral source. You then put that date on your calendar.

Let me show you how this works.

Let's say you do a community presentation (aka: *facilitation*). In your handouts, there is a feedback form where you invite people to sign up for your free newsletter. Then you send your newsletter out each month with informative articles on your topic to those that requested it. This is the simplest example of following through. If you do this religiously, you will have people calling saying, "I've been receiving your newsletter for months now and I think I want to come in."

Here is another example. Let's say you meet a possible referral partner at a networking event who says, "I'd like to know more about what you do." At the event, you get the person's card. When you get back, you enter that person's name and contact information into your contact management system. I recommend that you write them a "nice to meet you" note (by hand) or call them to schedule a meeting to talk. Enter the date of that contact into your contact management system. Then schedule the next time you wish to contact them and put that date on your calendar and under the person's name in your contact management system.

Ideally, you want to have regular contact with both prospects and referral sources so that your name is "top of mind" when needed. When I meet a new prospect or referral source, I enter their name into my contact management system. I like to plan the next six contacts with them. Then, I schedule those on my calendar so I know exactly when to contact them.

WISDOM NUGGET

By creating a system, your follow through can make your name "top of mind" when your prospect is "ready."

If you aren't connecting with your prospects and referrals sources, another therapist is.

Have a plan - whom do you want to connect with this week? This month?

When you connect with people you enjoy, it can be fun. I loving having lunch with my acupuncturist friend.

Coaching Questions:

1. Look at your income from the last six months. Where did your referrals come from? Might it be a good idea to reconnect with those referral sources?

2. If you were to make a list of 20 people, places or organizations that also serve your ideal client, who would be on that list?

3. Consider partnering with a colleague to keep each other on track as you create your "keep in touch" strategy.

CHAPTER THIRTY-NINE

What About Creating Products?

Recently a therapist client said to me, "I need to make more money, but not work more hours. What can I do besides raise my fees?"

There are only so many available hours we have to do therapy. Sooner or later you will fill up those hours. Then what?

How will you make more money? Do you have a zillion ideas about this? Is there a book or workbook in you?

It has been said that there are two ways to increase your income:

1. Get more clients.
2. Sell more to the clients you already have.

It's also 10 times easier to sell more to a client you already have than to find a new one.

Why not take some time during the natural lulls in your practice and decide how you might add value to your client's life (and make some passive revenue at the same time)?

Here are some ideas to get you thinking:

One summer, a fabulous therapist created relaxation CDs and when her clients found out about them, she sold out almost instantly. When she put them on a table after her community presentations on stress and overwhelm, they sold like hot cakes and resulted in some new clients.

One coach created a coaching workbook complete with practical and fun exercises. She sold it to her existing clients at a discount. They were excited to have something to support the work they were doing with her. She also sold it to prospects who couldn't afford individual coaching with her. Everybody felt good and she earned extra income.

Not only do these products give you some additional income, they give people the opportunity to know, like and trust you more. It gives them an experience of you so they can decide if they want to hire you.

You can also publicize these products on your website and offer them for sale or as a "freebie" to web visitors. It's a fact, by adding a simple audio message to your website, you can create more sales of your services.

Some people start to freak out and think this is too hard. But with today's technology, it isn't as hard as you might think. There are services that can help you do it easily.

Check out **www.CaseyTruffoRecommends.com** for a service that will help you easily create audio CDs you can sell.

WISDOM NUGGET

Stretch yourself. You have wisdom and knowledge to share. Package it and either give it away (as a marketing tool), or sell it to create some additional, passive revenue.

It's much easier than you think to create products. You don't necessarily have to rent studio time - you can create CDs and audio recordings right from your computer. With a little bit of technical support, you can put them on your website for free or for sale. You can also write a workbook that you can print or sell as an e-book on your website.

Coaching Questions:

1. What knowledge do you have that your ideal client would want?

2. How could you package and sell that knowledge?

3. Do you think you'd like to create that product? Or, is there a belief that might be stopping you? If there is, who can you talk to about it?

CHAPTER FORTY

Just Starting Out?

A common question I'm asked is, "Will this work for the new practitioner?"

Let me answer that by having Jodi Blackley, an MFT, in Fullerton, California share her story with you:

"I was licensed in January 2005. I went from zero to fifteen clients in one year. Now I'm regularly seeing sixteen to twenty clients a week and working towards seeing twenty-five clients a week."

I asked Jodi, "What practice building efforts did you try that did NOT work?"

"At first, I was encouraged to take practically any client who wanted my services, even at a sliding scale cost in order to get my name out there. When I did, I found myself getting extremely resentful. They would no-show or late-cancel and then not return. I learned not to do this.

"I also tried sending out letters to specific organizations. I'm fluent in ASL and attempted to contact organizations for therapeutic services for both interpreters and Deaf clientele alike. I did get some referrals, but they were all MediCal clients, and I don't take MediCal.

"I did a lot of cold emailing to lawyers by going through the Chamber email lists. I emailed practically everyone and waited to see who would bite. I met with a few family lawyers, but some asked about referral fees. Of course, I couldn't do that."

I asked her what DID work:

"I have learned to become more positive about my relationship with money and do not have a sliding scale, except to MFT interns from my Alma Mater.

"I am on a radio show once a month, which has come to be known as "Dear Jodi." People can call in or email questions, which I answer on the air. While it's not profitable, I'm not paying for the airtime - it's fun. I am getting quite a fan base. I will continue to do it as it is once a month. I Podcast all my shows, so people who visit my website can hear me - and the way I deal with issues. My Podcasts are listed on iTunes as well...the largest housing for Podcasts. Taking your words to heart of believing my practice is a business (and not a hobby) has been really important for me.

"I also believe in the 'Law of Attraction.' If my caseload suddenly drops off, I believe it's the world's way of allowing me to take a break and refocus my marketing efforts during my downtime. I've used your Vision exercise and a 'Law of Attraction' exercise so the vision of what I want is always in the forefront of my mind.

"BNI is just starting to work for me. I'm also part of other community-based networking groups that are non-therapist related. This keeps me constantly focused on marketing.

"Joining OC-CAMFT (Orange County chapter of California Marriage and Family Therapists) and now being part of the Board has helped me to find other therapists to partner with in marketing activities.

"Online marketing such as **PsychologyToday.com** has been an integral part of my income. My website **www.jodiblackley.com** has free 'tips of the week' which captures client information for me to send out a free relationship assessment.

"Networking with therapists from **PsychologyToday.com** has been a lot of fun and helped me to stay focused. We've met face-to-face over lunches and other gatherings, which provide a good referral base for one another.

"Supplementary, I joined a single insurance panel that has filled in the gaps in my schedule. I get a lot of clients from this one panel and I get paid quickly and without much hassle."

I asked Jodi how many hours a week she spends marketing her practice:

"Between working on my website, BNI, other networking ventures, etc., I'm putting in anywhere from five to ten hours/week."

What advice would she have for others?

"I would recommend that up-and-coming therapists first and foremost believe in themselves. Maintain the belief that "it" will happen if they persevere. Embrace business-building tools, and surround yourself with positive people, who are encouraging and willing to hear out your ideas...no matter how radical those ideas might be."

Realize that marketing is an integral part of the process and there are so many ways to go about it. You can pick and choose and determine what works for you. There isn't a "one way fits all" in marketing, which means flexibility and creativity.

"Finally, get your name out there. Not only to other therapists, but everyone. Therapists are only a small niche and if you're only marketing to other therapists, then you're missing out on the other 97% of the population. Networking groups are a dime a dozen and therapists haven't taken advantage of this precious resource to date. Therapists are starting to catch on though, so jumping on board now puts you ahead of the game."

I wanted you to hear Jodi's story. Clearly there isn't a "magic bullet" or "quick fix" to building a practice. You can see that Jodi is very committed to her vision of her private practice.

W I S D O M   N U G G E T

Rarely does one marketing strategy build your practice. You must try different things and see what works for you.

If you're just starting out and don't have a full practice, marketing your practice will be a part of doing business.

Accept it and find things you enjoy. It'll be something you need to do consistently.

And, just like Jodi, you can do it.

Coaching Questions:

1. What comes up for you when I talk about how marketing will be a necessary part of your business?

2. When you read Jodi's story, what ideas does it give you?

3. What three marketing activities will you commit to doing over the next three months?

SECTION EIGHT

Your Marketing Self Care Plan

"I once had a rose named after me and I was
very flattered. But I was not pleased to read
the description in the catalogue: no good in a bed
but fine up against a wall."
—ELEANOR ROOSEVELT

CHAPTER FORTY-ONE

Play for Keeps

When was the last time you took a day off just to do nothing? Not to catch up on paperwork or clean your house – just to recharge.

When was the last time you had a belly laugh so big that tears rolled down your cheeks? Are there hobbies you have let go of over the years because you are too busy?

Being self-employed can sometimes mean we forget to take time off. Without a doubt, we become better therapists, family members and citizens when we take time for ourselves. That is not selfish – it is self-supporting.

"Everyone of us needs to show how much we care for each other and, in the process, care for ourselves."
—Princess Diana

WISDOM NUGGET

Doing therapy can take its toll. After all, most of our work consists of dealing with people's difficult emotions. How do you "let down your hair?" When was the last time you did something just for you, something fun or playful or luxurious?

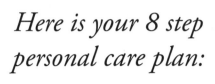

Here is your 8 step
personal care plan:

Laugh hard.
Play easy.
Do a little dance.
Smile up to your eyes.
Love with a light heart.
Take time for you.
Count your blessings.
Kiss a lot.

This chapter is purposefully short. Only one coaching question:

Will you plan regular time to get back to you – to reenergize your soul – to lighten up and rediscover the wonder in your world?

CHAPTER FORTY-TWO

Remember the Vision

There were some very dark days for me early on in my business. When I first started teaching therapists how to build their practices and told people my vision, they were pretty shocked with the concept of a *Wealthy Therapist.*

I want to teach therapists they can have a private practice that fulfills them and pays the bills with money left over for vacations and hobbies. I want to think of us not as "Poor Therapists," but "Wealthy Therapists" - wealthy in ways that far exceed money: Wealthy in time; in love; in the freedom to chose our clients; in following our calling to help people.

But as you can imagine, the concept of a Wealthy Therapist was threatening to some people. I was turned down for many years to speak at therapist's conventions. Hate emails came in regularly. Letters to the editor accused me of "gouging" clients. One lady even accused me of selling snake oil so I could become wealthy off the backs of poor therapists who "bought" my lies. To be honest, it hurt.

There were three things that keep me from throwing in the towel. First was my husband, Bob, who always believed in me and in my mission. He even retired so he could help me in the business. Second, was a small circle of dear colleagues who wouldn't let me give up.

Finally, there was the Vision. I knew this information needed to get out. It was critical for therapists starting a private practice to know how to do it. We didn't learn it in grad school as we discussed earlier. One couldn't successfully build a practice today, using methods that had worked in the past. If this information did not get out, I was concerned about the future of the profession. The average age of therapists is increasing and the average private practice income can't support a family of four. If this continues, no one will want to enter the profession.

The Vision. It's what got me up each morning. It's what keeps me going. The Vision.

Please allow yours to do the same for you.

WISDOM NUGGET

You're on this planet for a reason. Be open to your calling. And always, when the going gets rough, go back to the Vision.

Your Vision is what will keep you motivated.

Remember it daily. Savor it. Share it with others. Surround yourself with positive people who want you to be successful. But ultimately, your success is up to you.

Let your Vision be what propels you. We need you.

Coaching Questions:

1. Review your Vision. What do you want to do with your life on this planet?

2. When you look at your Vision, how do you feel? Are you excited and motivated or do you feel down? What do you need to do now?

3. I highly recommend sharing your highs and lows of practice-building with a trusted friend, mentor or coach. It's so easy to get caught forgetting what we need to remember - why we are called to be here. Who might you share with?

CHAPTER FORTY-THREE

Find Time to Market

"Perhaps the very best question that you can memorize and repeat, over and over, is, 'what is the most valuable use of my time right now?'"
—BRIAN TRACY, AUTHOR, MOTIVATIONAL SPEAKER

People often ask me, "How much time do I need to spend marketing my practice?"

My answer is, "At least one hour a day and four hours a day when you need a burst of clients."

The next question they ask is, "Where do I find that kind of time?"

1. Review your goals daily.

What is it you want? Have you written that down? It's so important to know what you really want and that you regularly review those goals to see if it's still what you want. Don't be afraid to remove goals that don't suit you any longer.

2. Establish your priorities.

Once you're clear on your goals, identify those that are the most important to you today. In terms of your practice, I recommend you prioritize your tasks by:

- Marketing activities that can bring you money today.
- Marketing activities that can bring you money in the near future.
- Marketing activities that can bring you money in the distant future.

3. Focus, focus, focus.

Clear your desk, computer and mind so you can focus on your priority number one task. If you have several projects out, and in sight, your focus will be diluted. (As I write this, I see that I need to do some more work on this one myself. My desk is covered with "very important papers.")

4. Eliminate distractions.

What distracts you from focusing? What do you need to do to eliminate those distractions? Turn off your email program during your marketing time. When my sister and I were kids, and my dad needed time to think, he'd say, "Stop. *Cone of Silence* time." The expression came out of that funny 1960's TV show, *Get Smart*. But my sister Pam and I would immediately be quiet. Do you need to put a *"Cone of Silence"* sign on your door so you aren't disturbed during your marketing planning time? Please don't try to multi-task unless you're more effective doing so.

5. Challenge yourself.

Do you remember that old game "Beat the Clock?" I play it all the time. I have a countdown timer. I set it for 30 minutes and then I see how many of my high priority tasks I can complete before the timer goes off. It's fun and I get so much accomplished.

6. Don't overbook yourself.

Each day is filled with unexpected surprises. Make sure you don't schedule yourself so tightly that these events cause you stress. The goal is to use the time you have to support your life and your goals.

7. Identify your accomplishments daily.

Review your successes and wins daily. Keep a "success journal" where you daily log every marketing activity you did or result you saw. Note how you spent your time. Was it in your best interest? Resolve to make the best use of your time each day.

I was once told, "You don't have to market your practice if you can't find the time to do so. You can continue to work in agencies if you like." The reality of that hit me like a ton of bricks and helped me start scheduling time to build my practice. I put that time on my calendar so I didn't book clients there and skip my marketing.

W I S D O M   N U G G E T

It's an illusion to think we can "manage time." We all have the same 24 hours a day. (Although if you figure out how to get more time in a day, that would be a fabulous specialty to market.)

As a former project manger, I used to say, "There are only two hard parts to a project - starting and finishing." It's easy to get distracted from starting (and finishing) marketing projects. So, make a list of what you'd like to accomplish this year - then this month - then this week. Reward yourself for each baby step you take. You can do this.

Coaching Questions:

1. What can you do right now to find the time to market your practice?

2. Remember a time when you did an outstanding job of marketing your practice. Why did you do so well? Can you repeat that success?

3. Are there changes you need to make in terms of how you spend your time now?

CHAPTER FORTY-FOUR

Focus on Completion
Not Perfection

My friend, Spencer, has been working at a hospital for over 15 years. 10 months ago he decided to open his private practice specializing in working with troubled teens. He now has office space and two clients so he's able to pay the rent. And that's just about it.

No matter what marketing effort Spencer starts, he finds himself stuck. He bought website hosting, but is still working on getting his website text "just right." He wants to meet with private school counselors, but wants to have a brochure done first. He has considered meeting with some psychiatrists who work with adolescents, but worries that they wouldn't really want to meet with him.

There are two phases in *starting* to market a private practice. First, you must find what you love and what will earn you money. Second, once you've found that specialty niche, you want to develop the words to use that will engage people in conversation or have them requesting more information from your website.

It's in the next phase, *implementing* the marketing plan, that a lot of therapists, like Spencer, get stuck.

When I explore it with them, I find it really is about a fear - a fear of getting out there and being rejected. So they don't get out there and market so they don't have to be rejected.

WISDOM NUGGET

When you begin to market your practice, a third of the people you talk to will be interested in learning more about what you do. A third of the people will be neutral and a third of the people won't care at all.

That's great news when you think about it. Once you know what to expect, it becomes easier. It means looking for the people that do care. Your mom told you that not everyone would like you. Well, not everyone will care that you're a therapist. Not everyone will care that you help people to feel and get better: sad but true. (Although, it's the same in other professions. I have met financial planners that love what they do. They help people make sure their money doesn't run out when they retire. That's pretty important. But when they talk about it – only one third are interested, "get it," and want to know more – the rest are either neutral or don't seem to care.)

But think of how many people "one third" is. If you talk to 100 people, that's 33 who want to know more. They won't all become clients right away, but you can get them into your "keep in touch" cycle. And then some of those, over time will become clients and some will become referral sources.

If you find yourself stuck, imagine what you'd do if you HAD to have a new client this week.

Take a step. Make a decision. Do something.

You'll find yourself moving pretty quickly once you get over the hump. It's all about completion - not perfection.

Coaching Questions:

1. In what areas do you find yourself struggling or stuck? What do you need to do in order to slip through the resistance and start moving again?

2. Do you think the fear of rejection or your perfectionism has impacted your marketing efforts? If so, what would you have to believe in order to change that?

3. Who might you call for support when you're struggling? Who is your cheerleader?

CHAPTER FORTY-FIVE

Be In On The Secret

In 2005, Rhonda Byrne began to study the 'Law of Attraction.' Within a year she had created the book and the full-length presentation, *The Secret*. It has attracted considerable interest from media figures such as Oprah Winfrey, Ellen DeGeneres, and Larry King. Many of my colleagues and I have been studying the Law of Attraction for years and enjoy the results we see in our lives.

So what is the Law of Attraction and how does it relate to practice building? First, let me ask you a question. How many times have you heard these quotes?

"Be careful what you wish for."

"Where your attention goes, your energy flows."

"If you think you're going to lose, you will lose."

Though they may not be referencing it, these people were talking about the universal Law of Attraction.

Simply put, the Law of Attraction is: what you think about - you create more of.

You can view this in spiritual terms, ("Ask and you shall receive") or as a universal law of quantum physics. The principle is the same: Focus on something and you often get it - whether you want it or not.

I was thinking about a former counseling client of mine. Many would say her life is great. She has a good job. She's in a doctoral program. She has the cutest puppy that's more like her child than her pet. But she never seems to get what she wants in life. School is too much work. She feels her bosses treat her unfairly. Week after week she shares her feelings of being unhappy and undervalued.

This reminded me of the times in my life where I felt like the victim. Especially when I didn't have enough clients to pay the rent. Every prospect that called was like "grocery money" and I really felt desperate.

The more desperate I felt, the less prospects called and the less money I had. My whole focus was on what I didn't have and then, guess what? I ended up with more of it.

I think learning to focus on what you want (and hope to have) is an ongoing process for most of us.

Here are the steps to help you focus on what you want:

1. Know where you're starting. In business, know your numbers. Know how many clients you have. Know how much money is coming in each month. Know your expenses.

2. Know what you don't want. Maybe you don't want to work with clients with eating disorders. Or children. There may be certain times of the day that you don't want to work. Be clear on what you really do not want in your life and your practice.

3. Be clear on what you do want. Imagine it. See it. Talk about it. Write it down. Create a "dream journal."

4. Clear out the resistance. Many people find that they can do the three steps mentioned above, but find that old beliefs (and naysayer(s) in their lives) keep them from really moving ahead. Do your own inner work to "clear the decks" for your success.

I know that as I moved away from poverty consciousness and began to slowly implement these steps, my practice started growing. This is one of the main reasons I love doing the work I do. As I help therapists to clear out the resistance and help them focus on what they want, magic seems to happen. Really!

WISDOM NUGGET

"In optimism there is magic. In pessimism there is nothing. In positive expectation there is thrill and success."
—ABRAHAM HICKS

What are you attracting? Focus more on what you do want. Keep a success journal with every good thing - big or small - that happens. Marty Seligman, the founder of Positive Psychology, suggests that to be happier, each day we should write down the three best things that happened to us that day - and why they happened. You just may find yourself happier, healthier and wealthier.

Coaching Questions:

1. Do you think that you attract more of "what is" when you focus on "what is?"

2. An important part of the Law of Attraction is "allowing" that which you desire to come into your life. Are you ready to "allow" greater joy and prosperity into your life? This sounds like a simple question so consider it for a bit.

3. There are many good books about the Law of Attraction. If you want to read more, consider *Ask And It Is Given* (or any of the books and audios) by Esther and Jerry Hicks and *The Law of Attraction: The Science of Getting More of What You Want and Less of What You Don't Want* by Michael J. Losier.

FINAL THOUGHTS

"The best is yet to be."
—ROBERT BROWNING

CHAPTER FORTY-SIX

What's Next?

It's my wish that, at this point you're feeling hopeful. However, I realize there is a lot of information in this book. Don't try to do everything at once or you will burn out faster than a broken sparkler.

I invite you to take a "big picture" look at the steps we have covered in this book. These are the building blocks for creating the practice you really want. But again, go slowly – it's not meant to be accomplished overnight.

Here are the topics we have covered. I encourage you to note which areas you need to review or take some action:

1. Money is not a bad word. (Sections 1 - 3)

Many of us learned early on that money was scarce or that we weren't going to get it. We entered this profession just wanting to help people and end up feeling bad about earning a good living doing just that. Do you need to review any old issues with money that might keep you from having the practice you really want?

2. Marketing is not ambulance chasing (or selling yourself out.) (Section 4)

You're not even selling your services. You're simply letting people in your community know you're there to help people in pain. In that way, you're doing your community a service by getting the word out about your practice. Do you have 'icky' feelings about marketing? If so, I invite you to review the chapters in Section 4. It might make sense to discuss them with your colleagues who don't feel as uncomfortable about marketing.

3. Your Marketing Personality and the Marketing Activities. (Sections 5 - 7)

All of us have different personalities and "one size" marketing plans don't suit everyone. Review these sections and find three marketing activities that you think might work. Start by making a copy of the Marketing Plan Checklist. Then take some action - no matter how small. Then track your results – see which marketing activities, over time, bring you clients. Do more of those activities.

4. Be true to yourself (Section 8)

Make sure you take time for yourself. Enjoy your life and the results of your practice building efforts - whether you have attracted 1 new client or 41 new clients. Success is success. I'm sure you've heard it said that, "success breeds success." Write down your daily successes (every day) in your "success journal."

WISDOM NUGGET

"We don't accomplish anything in this world alone."
—SANDRA DAY O'CONNOR.

---

5. Get support.

While private practice can be a lonely place, marketing one can be even lonelier. Please find a marketing buddy. Find someone with whom you can meet regularly to share your plans, efforts, opportunities, successes and challenges. This can be a family member, a colleague or a coach. Reach out. You don't have to do this alone.

Check out **www.BeAWealthyTherapist.com** for additional ways to stay on track and connected with like-minded therapists.

Don't let old issues with money or fears of marketing keep you from your dream. Start there.

Make sure you're looking forward to making a good living. Find marketing activities you enjoy and fit with your personality.

Design the practice you want. Then go after it.

CHAPTER FORTY-SEVEN

Final Coaching Questions to Propel You Forward

In each chapter I offered you some questions designed to challenge you. I wanted to offer you some additional questions to help you implement what you've read.

Some of these questions may be very important to you and some will be less so. Use the ones that suit you. But if you choose to skip some of them, consider why you're doing so and see if that reason makes sense. Sometimes it's the questions we most want to skirt that are the most meaningful to us. Have fun with them though:

1. Which sections of this book had the most impact on you? How so?

2. What are your thoughts on why therapists are some of the lowest paid healthcare professionals? Is there something you're called to do about it?

3. Earlier in this book, I asked you: On a scale of 1 to 10 (with 1 being 'very true' and 10 being 'very false,' how true for you is the statement, "Money is bad"? Let's take a checkpoint here and rank that statement again. Is your answer different than earlier?

4. Are there remaining issues with money that you need to work out? If so, how might you plan to do that?

5. How clear are you about your Vision? Practice? Lifestyle? Income?

6. As I did with the 'lack of chocolate cake incident', do you find yourself thinking, "There won't be enough for me"? If so, have you thought about what you might do to reframe that to more positive (abundance) thinking?

7. Have you set income goals for yourself? How much do you need to earn a week to make sure you have enough money for your expenses, your hobbies and your lifestyle?

8. What are your feelings about managed care and insurance panels? Where do they fit in your Vision? Did either of the chapters on insurance impact you in some way? If so, how?

9. On a scale of 1 to 10 (with 1 being 'very true' and 10 being 'very false', how true to you is the statement "Marketing is icky, unprofessional and bad"? Do you think that's different than before you started this book?

10. How do you feel about marketing a specialty to build your practice faster? Are there issues about this that you might discuss with a colleague? Have you picked a specialty niche where you'd like to focus your marketing efforts (a person, a problem or a person with a problem)?

11. What do you think of creating an ideal client profile and then taking your fictitious ideal client to Starbucks to really understand what he or she wants from you? Did that sound ridiculous or do you think it has some merit?

12. Of the Four Marketing Personality Types, which one do you most resonate with? Do you feel encouraged or overwhelmed by your marketing choices? If you feel overwhelmed, how will you break down some marketing activities into "baby steps" so you can have some fun with it?

13. Since the Internet will be an important place to market your practice in the decade to come, what will be the next step you take to improve your online presence?

14. As an experiment, I invite you to look at several therapists' profiles on the online therapist locators such as **www.Find-A-Therapist.com**, **www.Counsel-Search.com**, and **www.PsychologyToday.com**. Imagine you're a potential client searching these sites for a therapist. What attracts you? Do you like seeing the therapist's credentials ("Jungian therapist with extensive psychoanalytic background and eclectic style who loves doing sand tray work") or do you prefer to see how they might be of help to you with your problem? Additionally, I suggest you do this same assignment with therapists' websites. Pretend to be a potential client as you read the sites. See what draws you in and makes you want to know more.

15. You're in this for the long haul – not a sprint. What plans do you have to take care of yourself physically and emotionally during this process of building a practice?

16. Were there any case studies that resonated with you? Which ones and why?

17. Find your team. Who are your cheerleaders? Who is there to advise you? Who is there to help you with the technical or administrative work? Who is there to slow you down when you need it and to gently push you when you're scared to move?

18. What are your next steps? What can you do today to get started? How will you make time for marketing?

This final question is one I ask you with my whole heart so please receive it with the love and respect it holds for you:

How committed are you to building your private practice?

Your vision and your level of commitment will keep you going on the rough days. It's hard to do most things with very little commitment. Most of the clinicians that say, "I can't build a practice" really mean, "I have a low level of commitment." There is nothing wrong if building a private practice is "not your thing." But it's important to be honest with yourself. Either way, you do yourself a big favor with that honesty.

You deserve great things. So, what's next?

CHAPTER FORTY-EIGHT

A Final Story:
The Little Pink Rose

Once there was a little pink Rosebud, and she lived down in a little dark house under the ground. One day she was sitting there alone, and it was very still. Suddenly, she heard a little tap, tap, tap, at the door.

"Who is that?" she said.

"It's the Rain, and I want to come in;" said a soft, sad, little voice.

"No, you can't come in," the little Rosebud said.

By and by she heard another little tap, tap, tap on the window-pane.

"Who is there?" she said.

The same soft little voice answered, "It's the Rain, and I want to come in!"

"No, you can't come in," said the little Rosebud.

Then it was very still for a long time. At last, there came a little rustling, whispering sound, all round the window: rustle, whisper, whisper.

"Who is there?" said the little Rosebud.

"It's the Sunshine," said a little, soft, cheery voice, "and I want to come in!"

"N -- no," said the little pink rose, "you can't come in." And she sat still again.

Pretty soon she heard the sweet little rustling noise at the key-hole.

"Who is there?" she said.

"It's the Sunshine," said the cheery little voice, "and I want to come in, I want to come in!"

"No, no," said the little pink rose, "you cannot come in."

By and by, as she sat so still, she heard tap, tap, tap, and rustle, whisper, rustle, all up and down the windowpane, and on the door, and at the keyhole.

"Who is there?" she said.

"It's the Rain and the Sun, the Rain and the Sun," said two little voices, together, "and we want to come in! We want to come in! We want to come in!"

"Dear, dear!" said the little Rosebud, "if there are two of you, I s'pose I shall have to let you in."

So she opened the door a little wee crack, and in they came. And one took one of her little hands, and the other took her other little hand, and they ran, ran, ran with her, right up to the top of the ground. Then they said, --

"Poke your head through!"

So she poked her head through; and she was in the midst of a beautiful garden.

It was springtime, and all the other flowers had their heads poked through; and she was the prettiest little pink rose in the whole garden!

—From: *Stories to Tell to Children* by Sara Cone Bryant

Like the little pink rose, it's easy to hide inside our silence of our offices and wonder about where the next client is coming from. It's easy to feel nervous about the unknown - what will happen if you get out and market your practice? What will happen if you start charging a fee you feel better about? Please, for the sake of all of us, 'poke your head through' - let your wisdom and your passion shine. We need you. I challenge you to let those in your community get to know, like and trust you. Let them see your joy. Let them see what is possible.

I want to thank you again for having the courage to pick up this book and to allow me to share these tales with you. I am incredibly honored.

Please stay in touch. Let me know how you're doing. I want to hear your story. That's what keeps me on this mission.

I wish you great success. Happy practice building!

With love and blessings,

Casey

It has never been about selling yourself - it's about being the therapist you were called to be while earning a good and honest living doing it. Over and over in this book, I have written that you matter. You matter to me. You matter to your clients. You matter to the profession and to your community. Let the rest of the garden see how beautiful you are. Poke your head through.

"Working with Casey has been the most valuable and economical investment that I have made in learning how to establish a successful practice."

"Since my second month of being licensed, my practice has been full, which for me means between twenty-five to thirty-two clients a week. I love working with my client base, and I am not on any insurance panels. I can't imagine where I would be had I been able to apply all that she teaches in a logical, consistent way!"

- Piper Walsh, PhD

"Thanks to your techniques, I had 5 intakes in this past week! I used to average 1 per month."

"Who said niche marketing is limiting? I would have to say it's the on-going relationships with my referral sources. I'm glad I bit the bullet and dove into full-time private practice!"

- Jeannie Colvin
www.TherapyForTherapists.com

"Working with Casey has given me the courage to get off the insurance panels."

"Before I started consulting with Casey, I thought I'd never be able to free myself from my reliance on insurance companies. Today I've been able to build my business into a fee for service practice that I love. Thank you Casey for making this dream come true."

-Heather Tarlow-Edwards, Ph.D.
Psychologist, Marriage and Family Therapist
Orange County California Association of MFTs - Past-President

My Gift to You

Save **$50** on the
Be A Wealthy Therapist Implementation Kit.

A complete set of 12 Audio CD's AND 130-page workbook with all of the most important strategies to help you attract more clients now!

This self-study course includes 12 audio CDs (averaging 45 minutes each) and a 130-page manual called *How To Build Your Full and Rewarding Private Practice.* This is your "coach in a kit" and will take you through the steps in this book in much more depth. It's a good resource for motivated do-it-yourselfers!

Visit **www.BeAWealthyTherapist.com/bookreadersonly/** to activate your $50 discount. (There are CEUs available for certain states and licenses.)

Important Additional Resources

As I have said, our mission is to get the word out and to help you build your practice. Don't forget to check out what else is available.

Ready for some dedicated, personalized coaching to get your practice growing?

At **www.BeAWealthyTherapist.com,** we offer individual coaching packages designed to coach, train and support you in the 8 Key Strategies To Building The Practice You Really Want.

Whether you need a "tune-up" or want ongoing coaching where we look specifically at your challenges and opportunities, we have a program for you. You can read about the individual coaching programs we offer at **www.BeAWealthyTherapist.com/coaching.html**

After reading *Be A Wealthy Therapist,* **you may be hungering to connect with other success-minded therapists.**

You don't have to look far. Part of my mission is to create community.

Check out the *Build Your Private Practice Exclusive Members Program* at **www.BuildYourPrivatePractice.com.**

The Exclusive Members Program is a community of success-minded therapists, coaches, and healers who get together monthly in Tele-classes and in discussion forums to support one another, learn new marketing skills and stay focused on our practice-building efforts.

My partner, practice building coach Juliet Austin and I provide this group marketing training and coaching over the phone and Inter-net. If you're just starting out, or are on a budget, the membership program is the place to be.

We look forward to serving you.

Appendix A:
Your Personal Wealth Declaration

Recently I received a request for a donation from the local police and fireman's fund. In the envelope was a "Safety Declaration" card. It consisted of a few statements and a place for me to sign it and date it. For example, one statement said: I promise to obey the speed limit and drive in a safe manner.

Signing that card meant a lot to me. If I did so, I was promising to drive safely. While at first it sounds like a no-brainer, there is a part of me that really enjoys driving fast. I knew if I signed that card, I was promising and my word is important to me. Every time I am in the car now, I think about that card and the pledge. I am getting quite good at staying six car lengths behind the drivers in front of me!

Now it is your turn. On the next page you will have the opportunity to create your own Personal Wealth Declaration. I have included some suggestions but feel free to add your own declarations. Declare yourself. You can then cut it out of the book and put it a prominent place.

In fact, I am including two copies of the Personal Wealth Declaration. Feel free to pass one onto a colleague to spur each other on.

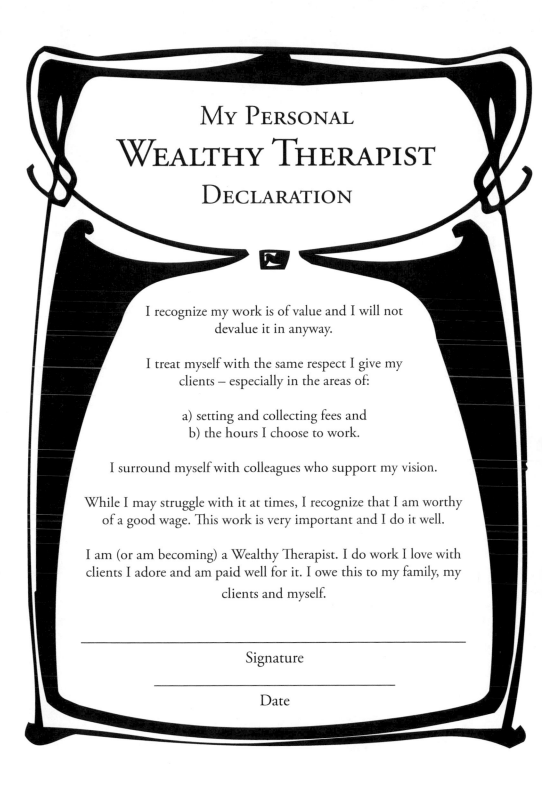

My Personal
Wealthy Therapist
Declaration

I recognize my work is of value and I will not devalue it in anyway.

I treat myself with the same respect I give my clients – especially in the areas of:

a) setting and collecting fees and
b) the hours I choose to work.

I surround myself with colleagues who support my vision.

While I may struggle with it at times, I recognize that I am worthy of a good wage. This work is very important and I do it well.

I am (or am becoming) a Wealthy Therapist. I do work I love with clients I adore and am paid well for it. I owe this to my family, my clients and myself.

_____

Signature

_____

Date

My Personal
Wealthy Therapist
Declaration

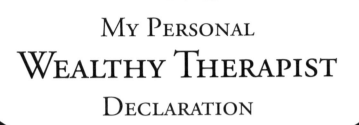

I recognize my work is of value and I will not
devalue it in anyway.

I treat myself with the same respect I give my
clients – especially in the areas of:

a) setting and collecting fees and
b) the hours I choose to work.

I surround myself with colleagues who support my vision.

While I may struggle with it at times, I recognize that I am worthy
of a good wage. This work is very important and I do it well.

I am (or am becoming) a Wealthy Therapist. I do work I love with
clients I adore and am paid well for it. I owe this to my family, my
clients and myself.

_____

Signature

_____

Date

Appendix B:
The Money Game Worksheet

In this worksheet, you will set your financial goals. You will discover how much you need to make per week, how many sessions you will need to do and how much you will charge to make the annual income you desire. Have fun. This is the Money Game.

Step 1: Identify what expenses you want the business to pay for. This is your Annual Income Goal.

a) Monthly Office & Business Expenses: $_____

b) Irregular Business Expenses (education, taxes, insurance, dues, etc): $_____

c) Home & Personal Expenses: $_____

d) "Extras" Money: $_____

e) Savings: $_____

f) Emergency Fund: $_____

_____

g) Total Annual Expenses (total a to f): $_____

Step 2: Now you know your Annual Income Goal. To reach that annual goal, you must know how much you need to earn a week. This is your Weekly Income Goal.

To determine how much you need to earn each week, divide your Total Annual Expenses (line g above) by 44. (We assume 44 weeks at full caseload.)

h) Weekly Income goal: Total Annual Expenses (line g above) ÷ 44 = $ _____

Step 3: Now you know your Weekly Income Goal.

The two variables that make up your weekly income are the number of sessions you do each week and your average session fee.

Step 4: Determine your current Average Session Fee.

Go through your calendar for the last six months. For each week, count the number of sessions you did and the income you billed for those sessions.

For each week, take the income you billed and divide by the number of sessions you did for that income. This will give you your actual average session fee. Here is a sample for four weeks to get you started. I recommend you do this every week from here on.

i) Week 1: Income ÷ Number of sessions = $ _____
j) Week 2: Income ÷ Number of sessions = $ _____
k) Week 3: Income ÷ Number of sessions = $ _____
l) Week 4: Income ÷ Number of sessions = $ _____

Step 5: Determine how many sessions you will need to do a week to make that weekly income goal (line h above).

Weekly Income Goal (line h) ÷ Average session fee (from line l above) = ____ # of sessions I need to do per week

This gives you a very realistic picture of your financial goals. You now know:

• How much you wish to earn per year.
• How much you need each week to make that annual goal.
• What your current average session fee is and
• How many sessions a week you need to do to meet your goals.

You are playing the Money Game.

Step 6: Track your progress and adjust as desired.

To increase your weekly income, you can either add more sessions per week or continually accept clients at higher fees so that your average fee goes up. By keeping track each week of your weekly income and average session fee, you stay on track toward your income goals.

If you want more specific instructions as to how to increase your practice, you may wish to consider the Be A Wealthy Therapist Implementation Kit. Visit page 323 to learn how to get your $50 discount for book readers only.

About the Author

CASEY TRUFFO fell in love with business as a youngster when her dad would take her to his office on Saturdays and let her play with the colored pencils and paper in the office supply closet. To this day, the smell of an office supply store can make her happily lightheaded.

She ventured into leadership at the age of 10 when she formed her first club.

There were two rules in the club:

1. Casey was the leader and;
2. Everyone in the club needed to obey the leader.
(For some reason, the club never really took off.)

Years later, at age 28, she became one of the youngest vice presidents of a major California bank. She has held senior management positions in the distribution and defense industries. When the defense industry took a hit in the late 1980's, Casey returned to grad school to pursue her Masters Degree in Marriage and Family Therapy. She was licensed in 1994 and went into private practice in 1996.

After figuring out the 8 Key Strategies to attracting therapy clients, Casey founded www.BeAWealthyTherapist.com. To date she has had the privilege of coaching therapists in 17 countries to value themselves and to build the private practices they really want. Her husband of nine years, Bob, retired from his job as a Financial Controller in 2004 in order to help Casey with her mission. Bob is the CFO of www.BeAWealthyTherapist.com. He's also in charge of accounting, shipping, receiving, purchasing, human resources and the laundry.

Casey and Bob currently live in Tustin, CA where Bob has an entire room devoted to his hobby - Lionel trains. The hobby they share is – Christmas. They work all year to prepare to put up the decorations on November 1.

For free audios, articles, marketing tips and to receive the email newsletter *Practice Builder,* please visit **www.BeAWealthyTherapist.com.**

To get in touch with Casey and the Be A Wealthy Therapist team, please visit www.BeAWealthyTherapist.com or email us at Support@BeAWealthyTherapist.com.

To contact us by phone: (949) 309-2590

Mailing address: 2212 Dupont Drive, Suite I
Irvine, CA, USA 92612

Don't forget - to get your $50 discount off the *Be a Wealthy Therapist Implementation Kit* (which includes 12 audio CDs and a 130 page self study manual entitled: *How To Build Your Full and Rewarding Private Practice*), go to:
www.BeAWealthyTherapist.com/bookreadersonly/

Special Appreciation

This book blooms from many hearts. On this page I want to thank my many teachers, mentors, colleagues, friends, family, clients and book shepherds that made my dream a reality.

To my Dad, who taught me I could be just about anything I wanted to be.

To Barb, who continually shows me how to love people.

To Muth, who had the greatest laugh and taught me how to sew.

To my sister Pam and her husband Billy. You have taught me to really enjoy life and to laugh at myself – which isn't too hard since I am only 5' 1" tall and have tiny ta-tas.

To Tiffany Truffo, thanks for continually teaching me about love, fun and style.

To my dear friend Maria Xanthos. Had it not been for you, Maria, I would still be scared to charge more than $50 a session. Your love and advice have been helped me have the business I've always wanted. I adore you!

To my "UberMentor" Andrea Lee. Andrea, you have touched my business and my heart. Thank you for helping me to find so many ways to live my mission and at the same time have a 'vacation lifestyle'.

To my right-hand Amber Miller, the best assistant that I have had in over 30 years in business. Amber, you're the best! Be A Wealthy Therapist runs smoothly because of you. I am very grateful.

To my friend and personal assistant, Kathy Derencin. You're the most beautiful and loving person I know. I am lucky and grateful to know you.

To Ellyn Bader and Pete Pearson. Thank you so much for encouraging, teaching and supporting me. And thank you for what you do for our profession. I treasure our friendship.

To my Be A Wealthy Therapist associate coaches: Arie Schwartzman, Cynthia McKenna and Harriette Lowenstein. You're amazing coaches and I feel proud to be a part of what you're doing. Daily, you make incredible differences in people's lives. I look forward to our future.

To my partner in the *Build Your Private Practice Exclusive Members Program* - Juliet Austin. You're a magnificent coach and a precious human being. I am so happy that we have joined together with this mission.

To the colleagues and mentors who have helped me and supported me from the beginning: Susie Duffy, Nancy Travers, Jory Adamson, Janeen Cunningham, Laurie Maroni, Elizabeth West, Lisa Henson, Margaret Schmitz, Dr. Barbara Brawerman, David Kuroda, Nora Ishibashi, Piper Walsh, Sydelle Tabrizy, Vondie Lozano, Sheri Zampelli, Suzan Aldimassi, Heather Tarlow-Edwards, Jill Sterling-Erman, Brett Williams, Marilyn Maher, Gary Robertson, Byron Perkins, Sandy Quinci, Lee Blackwell, Joe Devlin, Dennise Marie Keller, Christopher Keller, Graham White, Sue Williams, Lynn Grodzki, Nancy Sardella, Judy Westerfield, Linda Salazar, Judy Gifford, Melissa Groman, Simon (Yisrael) Feuerman and Chellie Campbell. You have helped me to be a better therapist, coach and person. Thank you.

To my wonderful "Book team"- especially my amazing editor Mike Flannery. He has taken my ramblings and made me sound almost coherent. Thank you so much, Mike, for fine-tuning this manuscript.

I want to thank the wonderful people at MP Press - Lynne and

Larry Klippel. You could be therapists by the way you encouraged me in the good days and kept me from tearing my hair out on a few occasions. You're wonderful.

To the fabulous team at www.Cyanotype.com - Sarah Van Male - who created the layout and cover design. What artists you are. Looking at the cover you created filled me with joy and gave me the energy to finish this book. Thank you.

To the terrific folks at Vervante. By fulfilling our orders, you have allowed me the time to concentrate on "spreading the word." Cindy, I am so grateful for all you and your team have done for us.

To those that have listened to me perseverate on these Money, Marketing, and Practice Building issues including my dear clients, members, and friends: I am in your debt.

To all counseling students, interns, and assistants, to therapists currently in agencies or hospitals, to anyone who dreams of starting a practice - I wish you great success. You can do it!

Above all, to my husband Bob who makes me smile everyday. I cherish our life together.